Brilliant

PowerShell

For

Beginners

South Crater Ltd

www.southcrater.com

Table of Contents

Table of Contents

Introduction

About the Author

The author of Brilliant PowerShell for Beginners is an IT professional based in the South East of England U.K. Writing ang blogging under the pseudonyms John Graham and the Practical Service Manager, the author seeks to share his knowledge and experience with over 25 years in the IT industry in Utility and Financial sectors.

Why I Wrote This Book

I wrote this book after many years using PowerShell in my day-to-day professional life as I think there is still a lot of confusion and misunderstanding surrounding the relative ease with which you can learn PowerShell and the extraordinary benefits which using PowerShell for IT Auto-ops can bring. My first experience with PowerShell manuals was an unwieldly 500-page volume that jumped straight into complex use cases and left me cold. In fact, it left me so cold that it was many years before I plucked up the courage to start again with PowerShell. In this book I have reflected upon the cmdlets that I use most often and the things I wish I had known when I got started.

Disclaimer

Whilst I am sharing my personal experience and knowledge, my publisher has asked that I include this disclaimer. This book contains hints and tips that I have picked up over the years. They may or may not be suitable for your organisation and your particular set of circumstances. Hence, this book is not intended to contain legal, financial, social, or technical advice.

You should procure the services of professional advisors where it is appropriate to do so. You are solely accountable for choosing to take any course of action. By continuing to read the content, you are agreeing that neither the author, not the publisher shall be liable for any costs, expenses, damages, or other losses occurring directly or indirectly from the use of, or reliance on any information contained herein.

How to use this Book

This book has been designed to flow logically from topic to topic but you can use it as a reference guide by reference to the table of content. Dipping in and out of topics as and when you need a reminder.

Code examples are highlighted in bold in a monospaced typeface and have been tested to work in PowerShell v5.x+

Where screenshots are provided to help convey a point, they are taken from a machine running Windows 10 and PowerShell 5. Your screen may look slightly different.

At the end of each topic is a section titled 'check your knowledge' where I pose questions for you to answer. The answers are all to be found in the text of this book. If you cannot answer any question at the end of the topic you should go back and re-read.

We Want to Hear from You

This book is published by South Crater Ltd, a small independent publisher of technical reference books. Proof reading and editing is managed in house.

We value your opinion and would like to hear your feedback. Feel free to get in touch to tell us what we are doing right, where corrections are needed or any topics you would like us to cover in future. Our email address is southcrater@virginmedia.com.

If you enjoy this publication, please leave a 5-star review on the online book store where you made your purchase.

We also welcome other approaches for collaboration on technical reference manuals or other training materials.

Getting Started

Topics covered in this section:

- What is PowerShell
- Running PowerShell
- Running as Administrator
- Execution Policy

At the end of this section, you will be able to:

- Start PowerShell and the PowerShell ISE
- Run PowerShell with elevated privileges
- Run PowerShell scripts saved on your computer

What is PowerShell

PowerShell is an object-oriented command-line shell and scripting environment for automating administrative tasks in Windows based environments.

It is a scripting environment and not a programming language. It is important you understand some of the differences between the two. Programming languages are generally complied as a one-time activity and then run as independent executables. PowerShell commands are interpreted at run time and require a host environment in which to run.

PowerShell is generally easier to learn than a programming language as most tasks can be completed in a few short specific lines of instructions. Do not be afraid of PowerShell, it can be quick to learn and powerful automation van be achieved in very few lines of code.

Running PowerShell

Most modern versions of Windows operating systems come packaged with PowerShell

PowerShell Version	Default Windows Versions
PowerShell 4.0	Windows 8.1 Windows Server 2012 R2
PowerShell 5.0	Windows 10
PowerShell 5.1	Windows 10 Anniversary Update Windows Server 2016
PowerShell Core 6	N/A
PowerShell 7	N/A

Table 1 - PowerShell Versions

PowerShell is part of the Windows Management Framework and can be downloaded and installed if it is not already packaged with your operating system.

There are several ways to start PowerShell. The simplest are:

1 – Search for PowerShell from the taskbar

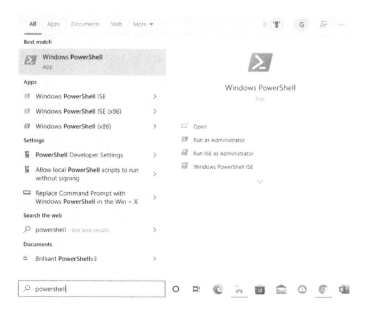

2 – Press the windows key and scroll to Windows PowerShell

3 – Open from Run menu. Press Windows R and type PowerShell

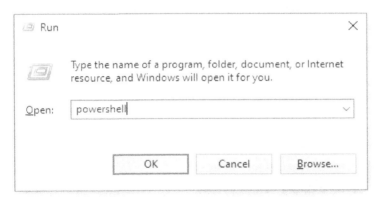

4 – From Command Prompt – Type PowerShell

```
Command Prompt - PowerShell
Microsoft Windows [Version 10.0.18363.1801]
(c) 2019 Microsoft Corporation. All rights reserved.

U:\>PowerShell
Windows PowerShell
Copyright (C) Microsoft Corporation. All rights reserved.

Try the new cross-platform PowerShell https://aka.ms/pscore6

PS U:\>
```

There are other methods such as running the executable from File Explorer, scheduling a task, or creating a desktop shortcut but these are the most common.

Version Installed

To check the version installed use the cmdlet Get-Host (see Jargon section for description of a cmdlet). The Get-Host cmdlet gets an object that represents the program running PowerShell.

Get-Host | Select-Object Version

```
PS U:\> Get-Host | Select-Object Version

Version
-------
5.1.18362.1801
```

Note the pipe character which is input by holding shift and pressing the backslash key on a UK/US QWERTY keyboard (the pipe is explained later in this publication).

Alternately query the variable hash table (more on variables and hash tables later)

$PSVersionTable.PSVersion

```
PS U:\> $PSVersionTable.PSVersion

Major   Minor   Build   Revision
-----   -----   -----   --------
5       1       18362   1801
```

PowerShell ISE

You may have noticed when searching for PowerShell there was also an option to open the PowerShell ISE. The ISE or Integrated Script Environment is a host application for running PowerShell that includes additional tools for testing and debugging your command scripts.

For a PowerShell beginner, one of the best features of the ISE if that it will make suggestions as you type meaning that you do not have to remember all the parameter names to a cmdlet.

In the example above, typing '-fore' will bring up the suggestion - ForegroundColor which can be selected with a double click to save typing it in full.

Furthermore, by typing a space, the ISE then brings up a picklist of colours to choose from.

Keyboard Shortcuts

Keyboard shortcuts are available in both the PowerShell application and ISE.

- Up arrow – cycles through last commands entered in PowerShell (In ISE used to move up between script lines)
- Home – Moves cursor to the start of the current line
- End – moves cursor to the end of the current line

- Tab – processing the tab key after entering the start of a Verb-Noun pair will cycle through matching commands (try it – type *get-AD* and then press tab a few times).
  - Note that if you type a full command in lowercase, pressing tab will correct the PascalCase.
  - Also useful to note, that if you type a command followed by space and a dash, the tab key will cycle through all parameters available e.g type *get-ADUser* – then press tab
- Ctrl and Home – deletes all characters from current cursor position to the start of the line
- Ctrl and delete - deletes all characters from current cursor position to the end of the line

Running as Administrator

You may also have noticed that launching PowerShell through the search bar gives an option to run as Administrator. It is not always necessary to run PowerShell as an Administrator and many commands will run without elevated privileges.

However, PowerShell is unable to participate in UAC User Access Control. That means when elevated privileges are required, PowerShell is unable to prompt for elevation. Instead, an error will be shown which might not make it obvious that admin privileges are needed.

It is good to remember that PowerShell cannot participate in UAC. When unexpected errors occur that cannot be fixed by any other method, try running with elevated privileges.

Some admins routinely open all PowerShell sessions as admin. Before doing so, you should be mindful of the security principle of least privileges. Always try to run with the lowest level of access required to achieve the task. Running a poorly written script with admin access can have devastating consequences.

Execution Policy

Often beginners try to start using PowerShell by running scripts found on the internet. Saving the script in their downloads file and then tying to open it in a PowerShell session will often throw up an error like:

```
Cannot be loaded because the execution of scripts is
disabled on this system. Please see "get-help about-
signing".
```

In this instance an execution policy has stopped the script from bring run. Execution policies are often thought of as a security boundary, but it is in fact just a simple method to prevent users from accidentally running malicious scripts. In a corporate environment, the execution policy is often set using a global policy object (GPO).

You can check the execution policy applied in PowerShell using the cmdlet

Get-ExecutionPolicy

The policy will be set to one of :

- Unrestricted – Allow all scripts to be run
- RemoteSigned - Allow local scripts and remote signed scripts to be run
- AllSigned - Allow only signed scripts to be run

As a user, you can override the execution policy without any elevated privilege. The simplest way to do so is to start PowerShell from a Command shell specifying that the policy is bypassed:

PowerShell.exe -ExecutionPolicy Bypass

There are other ways of bypassing the execution policy, like reading the script from a file and piping the commands into PowerShell but they are not as simple as just bypassing the policy.

Check Your Knowledge

 Can you describe at least 3 different ways to start PowerShell?

 Can you describe why you might use the PowerShell ISE?

 Why might you want to run PowerShell as Administrator?

 What is the Execution Policy?

PowerShell Lexicon

Jargon

PowerShell brings its own lexicon that can be confusing for a beginner. Let us look at some of the most common terms that you will come across.

Array

An array is simply a collection of multiple pieces of data. An array can contain one or more pieces of data or can be created as an empty array. (Arrays are covered fully later in this publication).

Cmdlet

A cmdlet is a command used in the PowerShell environment. Cmdlets perform an action and typically will return some output, usually in the form of a .Net object. The cmdlet name usually consists of a verb and noun pair.

Command

A command is just the invocation of a cmdlet. In fact, the terms cmdlet and command are often used interchangeably.

Hash Tables

A hash table is a specialised type of array that holds pairs of keys and values. (Hashtables are covered in more detail later).

Method

Methods are any actions that can be taken on an object. To find the methods for any object, pipe the object to the Get-Member cmdlet and select the Methods. For example

```
[System.String]$exampleObject = "A variable"
$exampleObject | Get-Member -MemberType Method
```

Module

A collection of cmdlets packaged for distribution.

Object

An object is a representation of something in the underlying .NET framework. An object has properties and can be acted upon using methods. An object's properties and methods can be viewed using the Get-Member cmdlet.

Parameter

Parameters are arguments that are passed to a cmdlet to influence the resulting processing or results. Parameters can be dynamic, that is to say they might change depending on a set of circumstances.

Pipe

To pipe, is to send the output of one cmdlet as an input to another. In PowerShell the pipe symbol is a vertical bar | or shift-Backslash on a QWERTY keyboard.

PowerShell Module

A PowerShell Module is a package that contains cmdlets. Modules must be installed in order for the cmdlets contained therein to be available. To get a list of installed modules use the Get-InstalledModule command.

Properties

Properties are the attributes or data that is associated with an object. An object's properties can be queried by piping the object to Get-Member cmdlet with -Membertype parameter set to 'Property'.

Script File

A script file is a file containing PowerShell commands saved with a .ps1 extension. The script file can be called and run in a PowerShell session manually or as a scheduled task.

Switch Parameter

A parameter that does not take an argument. Also referred to just as a switch. For example `-IncludeAll`

Syntax

The structure of a cmdlet along with its parameters or switches.

Variable

A variable is a value stored in memory that is represented by a text string prefixed with the dollar sign. (Variables are covered fully later in this publication).

Data Types

There are many different data types that can be accessed, set or otherwise manipulated in PowerShell. The basic types to be aware of when starting to script are:

Data Type	PowerShell Type	Description
Boolean		A true or false condition
Byte	System.Byte	Unsigned integer (whole number) from 0 – 255.
Character	System.Char	A Unicode 16 bit character. Example [char]0x263a is a smiley face ☺
DateTime	System.DateTime	A calendar date and time object. See Handling Dates later in this publication.
Decimal	System.Decimal	128 bit decimal value.
Double	System.Double	Double-precision 64-bit floating point number. 15-16 digits of precision. -1.79769313486232E+308 to +1.79769313486232E+308
GUID	System.Guid	Globally unique 32-byte identifier
Integer	System.Int32	32-bit signed integer
Long	System.Int64	64-bit signed integer -9,223,372,036,854,775,808 to +9,223,372,036,854,775,807
PSObject	System.PSObject	PowerShell object
Sbyte	System.Sbyte	Signed 8 bit integer -128 to 127
Short	System.Int16	Signed 16 bit integer -32,768 to 32,767
Float	System.Single	Single-precision 32-bit floating point number. 7 digits of precision - 3.402823E+38 to +3.402823E+38
String	System.String	Fixed-length string of Unicode characters
UInt	System.Uint32	Unsigned 32 bit integer 0 to 4,294,967,295
Ulong	System.Uint64	Unsigned 64 bit integer 0 to 18,446,744,073,709,551,615

| Ushort | System.Uint16 | Unsigned 16 bit integer 0 to 65,535 |

Remember you can check the type of any object by piping it to the Get-Member cmdlet or using its GetType() Method (where supported).

```
$example = "Text String" | Get-Member
```

```
$example = "Text String"
$example.GetType()
```

You can also check the minimum and maximum value formatting your query as follows (replace Byte with the type that you wish to query).

```
[Byte]::MinValue
[Byte]::MaxValue
```

15

Check Your Knowledge

Can you describe what is meant by these terms?

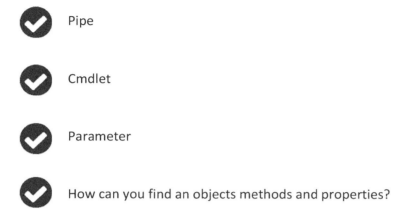 Pipe

Cmdlet

Parameter

How can you find an objects methods and properties?

Script Formatting and Layout

Topics covered in this section
- Case
- Readability
- Indentation
- Comments
- Spaces
- Backticks
- Splatting

At the end of this section, you will be able to

- Write well formatted PowerShell scripts

Case

In general terms PowerShell is not case sensitive. So, the variable $variableNew can also be referenced as $variablenew. Try it out

```
$variableNew = "hello world";
$variablenew
```

However, to make your scripts easier to read, especially when sharing with others, it is good practice to use standard capitalization structures that Microsoft implement in the .Net framework.

- lowercase – all lowercase with no word separation
- UPPERCASE – all uppercase with no word separation
- PascalCase - capitalizing the first letter of each word
- camelCase - capitalizing the first letter of the 2nd and subsequent words only

lowercase is used for keywords and operators e.g. -eq -like

17

UPPERCASE is used in comment-based help for emphasis. For example:

```
Get-Help -Name Write-Host

NAME
    Write-Host

SYNOPSIS
    Writes customized output to a host.

SYNTAX
    Write-Host [[-Object] <System.Object>] [-
BackgroundColor {Black | DarkBlue | DarkGreen | DarkCyan
| DarkRed |
    DarkMagenta | DarkYellow | Gray | DarkGray | Blue |
Green | Cyan | Red | Magenta | Yellow | White}]
```

PascalCase is used for all cmdlet names, parameters and function names e.g. *Get-Date*. A special case is however made for two letter acronyms that are always Uppercase e.g. the cmdlet *Get-ADUser* has the two-letter acronym for Active Directory in Uppercase.

camelCase is used for variable names, such as $variableName

Readability

Writing scripts that are easy to read is good practice as it makes it easier to debug, easier for another PowerShell scripter to make amendments and easier to understand what the script is doing.

Whilst PowerShell does not enforce any standards, here are a few tips that will help you maintain readability.

Indentation

When writing loops or conditional statements, it is good practice to indent each level. This will help you understand where each loop starts and ends.

This is especially important as you start to nest loops in your scripts.

See the example below:

```
[Int]$counter = 0
[Int]$varCountTo = 6
if ($varCountTo -lt 10) {
    Do {
        Write-Host -Object "Next Number is $counter"
        $counter++
    } While ($counter -lt $varCountTo +1)
}
```

Do not worry what this (nonsensical) script does, we will cover loops and variables later, for now just notice that adding indentation makes it relatively simple to see that there are two nested conditions.

Comments

You can also add comments to explain what each block is doing. There are a few different ways to add comments in PowerShell. The most common way to add a comment to a script is to prefix the line with a hash symbol #.

```
# Initialize the variables
[Int]$counter = 0
[Int]$varCountTo = 6

# check that the counter is set to stop at less than 10
if ($varCountTo -lt 10) {

        # Loop to count in increments of 1 until max count
is reached
    Do {
        Write-Host -Object "Next Number is $counter"
        $counter++
    } While ($counter -lt $varCountTo +1)
}
```

Adding a single space after the hash and leaving a blank line before each comment also helps with readability.

You can also add a block comment. A block comment consists of multiple lines of comments that start with the special symbol <# and end #>

```
<#
    This is a block of comments
    It is easier to read if each new line is indented
    by 4 space characters
    Keep each line short
#>
```

Block comments are commonly used in functions to provide usage examples.

```
Function Write-Example {
<#
    .SYNOPSIS
    This is an example function that displays the
username input

    .EXAMPLE
    Write-Example<<username>>
#>
param (
    $userName
)
Write-Host "You called this function with username
$userName"
}
```

It is also possible to add comments in line with code. This is not recommended as it can cause confusion as to whether code on the line is executed or just commented.

If in-line comments are used, then leave at least 4 space characters between the end of the code and the start of the comment, to make it obvious where the code end and the comment begins.

See the example on the next page:

```
$MailMessage = @{
    To = "recipient@yourcompany.com"
    From = "sender@mycompany.com"
    Subject = "Test Email"
    Body = "This is a test email"
    Smtpserver = "smtphostserver"
    ErrorAction = "SilentlyContinue"      #supress error
messages and continue
}
```

Spaces
Readability can be greatly improved using whitespace. You will have seen in the examples above that adding blank lines before comments and the use of indents greatly improves readability.

Additionally, you should use a single space character around parameter names and operators, including comparison operators and math and assignment operators. Theses paces are not strictly necessary for PowerShell to parse your code but again improve readability.

For example

```
$inputVar = Get-Content -path $filePath -Wait: (
$ReadCount -gt 0) -First ( $ReadCount * 5)
```

Backticks
Often you will use a PowerShell command which can be written as a single line. For example, the code below will find the free space on a local machine. It is a long command and very hard to read

```
Get-CimInstance -ComputerName localhost win32_logicaldisk
| where caption -eq "C:" | foreach-object {write "
$($_.caption) $('{0:N2}' -f ($_.Size/1gb)) GB total,
$('{0:N2}' -f ($_.FreeSpace/1gb)) GB free "}
```

Backticks can be used to break up the command over several smaller lines. For example:

```
Get-CimInstance -ComputerName localhost win32_logicaldisk
`
| where caption -eq "C:" `
| foreach-object {write " $($_.caption) $('{0:N2}' `
-f ($_.Size/1gb)) GB total, $('{0:N2}' `
-f ($_.FreeSpace/1gb)) GB free "}
```

The backtick character (top left of the QWERTY keyboard, to the left of the number 1 key) tells PowerShell that the command word-wraps across the line.

Whilst it makes code easier to read, there are issues with the use of the back-tick that has meant it has fallen out of favour, the biggest issue is that any whitespace after the tick can cause the command to fail.

In the example above, the tick is not really needed on every line. Instead, the line can be broken at the pipe character or an opening brace. PowerShell is intelligent enough to know that there is more content required after the pipe or brace character so continues to read the next line before interpreting the command. Carefully breaking the line can remove the need for most of the backticks.

Can you spot the one remaining backtick?

```
Get-CimInstance -ComputerName localhost win32_logicaldisk
|
where caption -eq "C:" |
foreach-object {
write " $($_.caption) $('{0:N2}' -f ($_.Size/1gb)) GB
total, $('{0:N2}' `
-f ($_.FreeSpace/1gb)) GB free "
}
```

Splatting

Another technique to break commands across lines and improve readability is known as splatting. Splatting is a technique to pass a set of parameters to a cmdlet as a single unit. The parameters are usually held in a hash table (more on hash tables later).

For example, to copy a file from one location to another, you can write the command as

```
Copy-Item -Path "OrignalFile.txt" -Destination
"CopiedFile.txt" -WhatIf -Force
```

Alternatively, you could use back ticks to break the command into easier to read chunks:

```
Copy-Item `
    -Path "OriginalFile.txt" `
    -Destination "CopiedFile.txt" `
    -WhatIf `
    -Force
```

But as backticks are out of style due to the issues with additional white space or ease with which it is possible to miss a backtick from a line, splatting is the better method to break up this command.

```
$Params = @{
   "Path" = "OriginalFile.txt"
   "Destination" = "CopiedFile.txt"
   "WhatIf" = $True
   "Force" = $True
}
Copy-Item @Params
```

Check your knowledge

Can you explain when you would use:

 lowercase

 PascalCase

 camelCase

 Why is it best not to use backticks?

 What is splatting used for?

Hello World

Topics covered in this section

- First script to write a message to the host console
- Cmdlet verbs

At the end of this section, you will be able to

- Write and run a simple PowerShell script
- Understand the cmdlet verb-noun pair
- Use cmdlet parameters

Hello World

Like all good scripting guides, we will start with the ubiquitous lesson to display the message "Hello World". It looks simple right, so why start so basic? Well, as simple as it looks, this script will teach you the basic syntax of PowerShell and more importantly is a useful test that you have PowerShell installed and running correctly.

Open your favourite text editor and type in the command

Write-Host -Object "Hello World" -ForegroundColor Red - BackgroundColor White

Save the file as 'c:\temp\sayhello.ps1'

Now open PowerShell, remembering to bypass the execution policy if you need to (in CMD shell type **PowerShell.exe -ExecutionPolicy Bypass**).

To run the script, you need to specify its location and name.

c:\temp\sayhello.ps1

Note that PowerShell does support shortening this to :- .\ sayhello

.\ is shorthand for current location (ensure that you are in the right folder) and the .ps1 extension is not strictly necessary. However, we are writing brilliant PowerShell so will specify the full path and filename.

The command in your new script file will output the message 'Hello World' in red text on a white background.

Breaking the command down, we can see that the cmdlet name is

'Write-Host'. Like all PowerShell cmdlets it consists of a verb-noun pair.

The verb 'Write' defines the action, to write the output.

The Noun 'Host' identifies the object on which is the action is performed, the message is written to the host console.

Commonly used verbs include:-

Verb	Action
Add	Adds a resource to a container or attaches an item to another item.
Clear	Removes all the resources from a container but does not delete the container.
Close	Changes the state of a resource to make it inaccessible
Copy	Copies a resource to another name or to another container.
Find	Looks for an object in a container that is unknown, implied, optional, or specified.
Get	Retrieves an object
Hide	Makes a resource undetectable.
New	Creates a new object
Open	Changes the state of a resource to make it accessible
Set	Sets property on an object
Show	Makes a resource visible to the user.
Unlock	Releases a resource that was locked.

Table 2 Common Verbs

It is also worth noting that nouns are always stated in the singular form. For example, you might want to Get all running Services. If you write the command as Get-Services you will see an error "The term 'get-services' is not recognized as the name of a cmdlet, function, script file, or operable program". Get-Service (with Service in the singular form) would return all running services.

The cmdlet accepts parameters. In the example script we have defined the object to write as a literal string and the foreground and background colours. Note that the literal string can be enclosed in either single or double quotes. In PowerShell single and double quotes are interchangeable but it is worth nothing that double quotes will force all variables to be replaced with their value. See it for yourself with these commands

```
$message = 'hello World'

# Single Quotes
Write-Host -Object 'message says - $message'

# Double Quotes
Write-Host -Object "message says - $message"
```

The cmdlet accepts other optional parameters. The full syntax for any cmdlet can be displayed using the Get-Help command.

For example *Get-Help -Name Write-Host* returns the following information (shortened for the purpose of this publication):

```
NAME
    Write-Host

SYNOPSIS
    Writes customized output to a host.
```

SYNTAX
```
    Write-Host [[-Object] <System.Object>] [-
BackgroundColor {Black | DarkBlue | DarkGreen | DarkCyan
| DarkRed |
    DarkMagenta | DarkYellow | Gray | DarkGray | Blue |
Green | Cyan | Red | Magenta | Yellow | White}]
    [-ForegroundColor {Black | DarkBlue | DarkGreen |
DarkCyan | DarkRed | DarkMagenta | DarkYellow | Gray |
DarkGray
    | Blue | Green | Cyan | Red | Magenta | Yellow |
White}] [-NoNewline] [-Separator <System.Object>]
    [<CommonParameters>]
```

See the section 'Understanding Syntax' for a full explanation of the SYNTAX section.

You may also have noticed that, as we write brilliant PowerShell, we have both purposely used the verbose form of the cmdlet and have used PascalCase (capitalizing the first letter of each word) for the cmdlet name and parameters. The following command works (but is not as well formed).

```
write-host 'Hello World' -foregroundcolor red -
backgroundcolor white
```

Check your knowledge

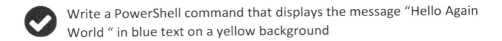 Write a PowerShell command that displays the message "Hello Again World " in blue text on a yellow background

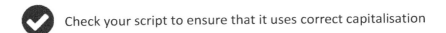 Check your script to ensure that it uses correct capitalisation

 Save your commands as a script file and run the file.

Getting Help

Topics covered in this section

- Getting help with get-Help
- Updating help files
- Finding commands with get-Command
- Understanding help syntax
- Common cmdlet parameters
- Risk management parameters

At the end of this section, you will be able to

- Find commands, get and understand help files
- Use command and risk management parameters

Get-Help

Fortunately, you do not need to remember the exact parameter and syntax of every PowerShell command. There are two cmdlets that you can use to get help. Get-Help and Get-Command.

The Get-Help cmdlet displays information about PowerShell concepts and commands, including cmdlets, functions, Common Information Model (CIM) commands, workflows, providers, aliases, and scripts.

To get basic help for a cmdlet type *Get-Help -Name <<cmdlet>> For example Get-Help -Name Get-Help.* This will return details including:

- Name
- Synopsis
- Syntax
- Description
- Related Link
- Remarks

Useful switches include

- *-Examples* to display examples of how to use the cmdlet
- *-Detailed* Adds parameter descriptions and examples to the basic help display
- *-Full* Displays the entire help article for a cmdlet

Help can also be accessed by typing `Help -Name <<cmdlet>>`

Help -Name <<cmdlet>> is a function that runs get-help and displays the output a page at a time. Press enter to step through the details.

Update-Help

Help file are stored on your local machine in the PowerShell installation directory (e.g. C:\Windows\System32\WindowsPowerShell\v1.0\en-US).

Your installation directory is held in a social variable $PSHome (type $PSHome in PowerShell and you will see the full path displayed)

As it is stored locally, the information held becomes stale and occasionally you will see a message to advise that help is not available or incomplete:

"Get-Help cannot find the Help files for this cmdlet on this computer. It is displaying only partial help. -- To download and install Help files for the module that includes this cmdlet, use Update-Help."

To update the help files on your machine, use the cmdlet *Update-Help.* Your machine will need to be connected to the internet.

Update-Help checks the version of the help files on your computer. If you do not have help files for a module or if your help files are out of date, the newest versions are downloaded and saved.

Online Help

You can view the most up-to-date helpfiles online in the Microsoft Documentation portal. Search 'PowerShell <<Command>>' in your favourite search engine or in powershell use the -online switch to Get-Help. For example

Get-Help -Name Get-Command -Online

Get-Command

Get-Command is designed to help you find commands. Used without any parameters, the Get-Command cmdlet will return a list of all cmdlets and functions installed on your machine.

Get-Command supports the use of wildcard characters. Hence:

Get-Command -Name Update-Storage*

Will return all commands that start Update-Storage

CommandType	Name	Version	Source
Function	Update-StorageFirmware	2.0.0.0	Storage
Function	Update-StoragePool	2.0.0.0	Storage
Function	Update-StorageProviderCache	2.0.0.0	Storage

Get-Command with the full name of a cmdlet will display details of that cmdlet and import the module so that the command can be used straight away. You will notice that the details displayed are not as detailed as those when using Get-Help.

Use the switch -Syntax to show the command syntax

Get-Command can also be used to find all verbs can be performed on a Noun (remember cmdlets are Verb-Noun Pairings). Try it now:

Get-Command -Noun Process

Understanding Syntax

When you first look at a command's syntax, it can be very confusing. The following snippet is returned by Get-Help -Name Stop-Process

```
Stop-Process [-Id] <System.Int32[]> [-Force] [-PassThru]
[-Confirm] [-WhatIf] [<CommonParameters>]
```

Syntax of Syntax

To start, it is helpful to understand the syntax of syntax.

Character	Description	Meaning
< >	Angle Brackets	Angle brackets are used for placeholder text that identify the .NET type of the value that a parameter takes. You do not type angle brackets but instead replace the with an item of the type described e.g replace <<System.Int32> with a 32-bit signed integer.
-	Hyphen	Indicates a parameter name or switch (Remember a switch parameter is a parameter with no value) -Id is a parameter to Stop-Process
[ ]	Square Brackets	Square brackets are used to indicate that an item is optional. [-Id] is therefore an optional parameter. Square brackets at the end of a .NET type indicates that one or more values can be entered (separated with a comma) e.g. System.Int32[] indicates one or more 32-bit integers can be passed as arguments to the parameter.
{ }	Braces	Braces represent a choice. The values within braces are separated by vertical bars to indicate an OR choice. E.g. -Option {None | ReadOnly | Constant | Private | AllScope}

Table 3 - Syntax

The table can therefore be summarised thus:

    <command-name> -<Required Parameter Name> <Required Parameter Value>

    [-<Optional Parameter Name> <Optional Parameter Value>]

    [-<Optional Switch Parameters>]

    [-<Optional Parameter Name>] <Required Parameter Value>

It is useful to commit that to memory, but should you need a reminder, use the command *help about_command_syntax*

Going back to **Get-Help -Name Stop-Process**

- **Stop-Process -** is the command name
- **[-Id] <System.Int32[]>** - the parameter name is optional but one or more values are expected, comma separated
- **[-Force]** – is an optional switch
- **[-PassThru]** – is an optional switch
- **[-Confirm]** – is an optional switch
- **[-WhatIf]** – is an optional switch
- **[<CommonParameters>]** – is an optional set of common parameters (covered later in this chapter)

Get-Help -Name Stop-Process actually returns three different syntax cases. That is because the cmdlet can be used in three different ways to stop a process by its Id, Name or InputObject.

InputObject in this case is a running process object, referenced in a variable. Consider the script below:

```
$procToStop = Get-Process -Name "WinWord"
Stop-Process -InputObject $procToStop
```

The variable $procToStop contains the InputObject to stop, in this case Microsoft Word.

InputObject can also refer to the pipeline of objects from a query. The pipeline is covered in more detail in the later section 'the Pipeline'.

Common Parameters
Common Parameters can be used with almost any cmdlet.

- [-Debug] Switch displays detailed developer level information about the code being executed.
- [-ErrorAction <Break|Suspend|Ignore|Inquire|Continue|Stop|SilentlyContinue>] Defines what to do in the event of a non-terminating error
- [-ErrorVariable <System.String>] Defines variable in which to hold error messages about the command being executed (in addition to the automatic variable $error).
- [-InformationAction <Break|Suspend|Ignore|Inquire|Continue|Stop,|SilentlyContinue>] Defines how information messages are handled.
- [-InformationVariable <System.String>] Defines variable that holds information messages generated by Write-Information command
- [-OutVariable <System.String>] Defines a variable to store output objects as well as sending them to the pipeline
- [-OutBuffer <System.Int32>] Defines number of objects to cache before sending along the pipeline
- [-PipelineVariable <System.String] Defines variable to store the current pipeline element as a variable
- [-Verbose] Switch displays detailed information about the command being executed (when the command generates a verbose message)
- [-WarningAction <Break|Suspend|Ignore|Inquire|Continue|Stop,|SilentlyContinue> Defines action to take when a warning is generated by a command
- [-WarningVariable < System.String>] defines variable to store the warning message

All common parameters are implemented by PowerShell but may not be supported by the developer of the cmdlet. That's means that they are always accepted as input to a cmdlet but the performance and outcome might not always be as expected. For example, the switch -Verbose might not have any effect at all if the cmdlet is not coded to generate verbose output.

Risk Management Parameters

Some PowerShell cmdlets and functions introduce commands that carry risk. For example, the command Stop-Process can cause instability on a system by stopping a running process. These commands often support two special risk management parameters Confirm and WhatIf.

-Confirm prompts for user confirmation before performing an action

```
PS U:\> Stop-Process -InputObject $procToStop -Confirm

Confirm
Are you sure you want to perform this action?
Performing the operation "Stop-Process" on target "WINWORD (6000)".
[Y] Yes  [A] Yes to All  [N] No  [L] No to All  [S] Suspend  [?] Help (default is "Y"):
```

-WhatIf displays a message to confirm what the command would have done but does not execute it.

```
PS U:\> Stop-Process -InputObject $procToStop -WhatIf
What if: Performing the operation "Stop-Process" on target "WINWORD (6000)".
PS U:\>
```

Check your knowledge

 Find all commands that start 'Get-Storage'

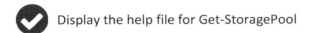 Display the help file for Get-StoragePool

 How many -UniqueId can be specified for Get-StoragePool

 What switch would add to your script to prompt user confirmation?

Understanding Modules

Topics covered in this section

- What is a module
- Installing modules
- Importing modules

At the end of this section, you will be able to

- Check modules installed
- Instal and use PowerShell modules

What is a Module

In simple terms a module is a collection of objects including PowerShell cmdlets that a developer has packaged for distribution to users.

Not all PowerShell cmdlets are installed in the base product as part of your operating system. Specialized modules are separately distributed and can be installed and imported as required.

Examples of available modules include:

- Active Directory
- SQL
- ExchangeOnline
- SharePoint Online
- Azure

Once installed and imported, cmdlets in the module are available to use.

Using the Get-Command cmdlet with wildcard characters, we can find the Commands and Functions relating to Modules (remembering that the Noun Module is used in singular form).

`Get-Command -Name *-Module`

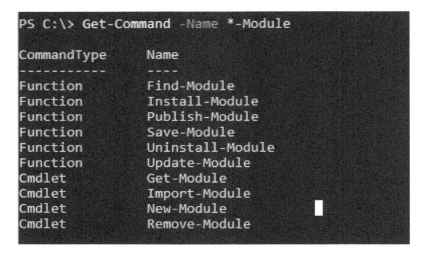

```
PS C:\> Get-Command -Name *-Module

CommandType      Name
-----------      ----
Function         Find-Module
Function         Install-Module
Function         Publish-Module
Function         Save-Module
Function         Uninstall-Module
Function         Update-Module
Cmdlet           Get-Module
Cmdlet           Import-Module
Cmdlet           New-Module
Cmdlet           Remove-Module
```

You might be tempted to use Get-Module to find all modules installed but a quick look at the help for this command shows that Get-Module with no parameters only returns modules imported into the current session.

To find all modules available use the switch -ListAvailable

`Get-Module -ListAvailable`

The output will show modules available and the commands in each module.

```
    Directory: C:\WINDOWS\system32\WindowsPowerShell\v1.0\Modules


ModuleType Version    Name                    ExportedCommands
---------- -------    ----                    ----------------
Manifest   1.0.1.0    ActiveDirectory         {Add-ADCentralAccessPolicyMember, Add-ADComputerServiceAcc.
Manifest   1.0.0.0    AppBackgroundTask       {Disable-AppBackgroundTaskDiagnosticLog, Enable-AppBackgro.
Manifest   2.0.0.0    AppLocker               {Get-AppLockerFileInformation, Get-AppLockerPolicy, New-Ap.
Manifest   1.0.0.0    AppvClient              {Add-AppvClientConnectionGroup, Add-AppvClientPackage, Add.
Manifest   2.0.1.0    Appx                    {Add-AppxPackage, Get-AppxPackage, Get-AppxPackageManifest.
Script     1.0.0.0    AssignedAccess          {Clear-AssignedAccess, Get-AssignedAccess, Set-AssignedAcc.
```

Conversely, the Get-Command cmdlet will display the module that any given command is installed by.

```
PS C:\> Get-Command -Name *-Module

CommandType     Name                                      Version    Source
-----------     ----                                      -------    ------
Function        Find-Module                               1.0.0.1    PowerShellGet
Function        Install-Module                            1.0.0.1    PowerShellGet
Function        Publish-Module                            1.0.0.1    PowerShellGet
```

The column 'Source' displays the source module. Check by searching for the module PowerShellGet

Get-Module -ListAvailable | Where-Object Name -eq PowerShellGet

```
PS C:\> Get-Module -ListAvailable | Where-Object Name -eq PowerShellGet


    Directory: C:\Program Files\WindowsPowerShell\Modules


ModuleType Version    Name                                ExportedCommands
---------- -------    ----                                ----------------
Script     1.0.0.1    PowerShellGet                       {Install-Module, F
```

You may have noticed the Column ModuleType when looking at available module. You need not worry about the module type at this stage, but for the curious they are detailed below.

Script Modules
Any script file save as a PSM1 files that contains mainly functions and code, used by script developers and administrators.

Binary Modules
Contain compiled code, based on a .NET Framework assembly (DLL), used by cmdlet developers to create modules containing cmdlets.

Manifest Modules
Script modules containing a manifest file to describe all its components e.g. information about the author.

Dynamic Modules
A special type of module that exists only in memory, created using the New-Module cmdlet. Members of the dynamic module (functions/variables) are immediately available in the PowerShell session until the session is closed.

41

Installing Modules

PowerShell Gallery

The simplest way to install a PowerShell module is form the PowerShell Gallery. The PowerShell gallery is an online repository for sharing PowerShell modules and scripts. Us the command Find-Module with no parameters to list all modules available in the gallery but beware – at the time of writing this page there were over 9,000 modules and scripts available.

Find-Module supports wildcard characters

```
Find-Module -Name SQL*
```

Will return all modules in the gallery with a name starting SQL.

Alternatively use **Find-Module -Filter SQL** to search for the string 'SQL'in the module name, description, and tags.

Once you have found the module to install (using one of the commands above, using Get-Command to show the module source or just through searching the internet), Install the module using the cmdlet Install-Module

```
Install-Module -Name SqlServer
```

Note that you will usually require Administrator Rights to install modules.

Use the optional parameter **-MinimumVersion <String>** if you want to specify the minimum version number to install.

In the background, the NuGet provider manages the installation. You do not need to understand NuGEt at this stage, but it is referenced here in case you see an error message like "Do you want PowerShellGet to install and import the NuGet provider now?" If you see this message click Y to continue.

Manual Install

If you want to install a module that is no longer in the PowerShell Gallery and you can obtain it from a different source, the module can be installed manually.

Firstly, you need to find the path to save the module to. Fortunately the path is held in an environment variable and can be displayed in PowerShell with the command **$ENV:PSModulePath**

The PSModulePath will usually return three or more paths that look like this:

```
C:\Users\<<username>>\Documents\WindowsPowerShell\Modules
C:\Program Files\WindowsPowerShell\Modules
C:\WINDOWS\system32\WindowsPowerShell\v1.0\Modules\
```

Choose the first path if you want to install the module and make it available for just the current logged in user.

Choose the second path to make it available for all users on the machine.

The third path is where modules built-in to the operating system are stored and it is recommended not to use this path.

Whilst it is possible to install modules in other locations, it's easier to use one of the predefined paths as PowerShell knows to look here.

Save your module to the preferred path and then check it is available using

`Get-Module`

Import-Module

As of PowerShell 3.0 modules will be imported automatically when you use any command contained in that module. However, you can manually import the module to check your installation using the command Import-Module

Check your knowledge

 How would you find all modules available to use?

 Can you find the path where modules are installed?

 Using the -WhatIF switch try to install any module and check the result.

Objects, Properties & Methods

Topics covered in this section

- Objects
- Methods
- Properties

 At the end of this section, you will be able to

- Identify any objects type
- Find the methods and properties for any object

Objects

An object is a collection of data (known as members) that form a representation of something in the underlying .NET framework. An object has properties and can be acted upon using methods.

Almost everything that you interact with in PowerShell is an object. For example, the command Get-Service returns objects that represent the services (running and stopped) on a machine.

Every object has a type. The object type is displayed as the first line when the object is piped to the Get-Member cmdlet.

```
PS C:\> Get-Service | Get-Member

   TypeName: System.ServiceProcess.ServiceController
```

It is useful to know the object type as we can use that to find the cmdlets that accept the type as an input parameter.

```
Get-Command -ParameterType
System.ServiceProcess.ServiceController
```

```
PS C:\> Get-Command -ParameterType System.ServiceProcess.ServiceController

CommandType     Name                    Version    Source
-----------     ----                    -------    ------
Cmdlet          Get-Service             3.1.0.0    Microsoft.PowerShell.Management
Cmdlet          Restart-Service         3.1.0.0    Microsoft.PowerShell.Management
Cmdlet          Resume-Service          3.1.0.0    Microsoft.PowerShell.Management
Cmdlet          Set-Service             3.1.0.0    Microsoft.PowerShell.Management
Cmdlet          Start-Service           3.1.0.0    Microsoft.PowerShell.Management
Cmdlet          Stop-Service            3.1.0.0    Microsoft.PowerShell.Management
Cmdlet          Suspend-Service         3.1.0.0    Microsoft.PowerShell.Management
```

From the screenshot above you can see the cmdlets that accept a
ServiceController as an input param. Let us have a closer look at Stop-Service.
Remember you can use Get-Help to find out more about the syntax for any
command. **Get-Help -Name Stop-Service** returns the following:

```
SYNTAX
    Stop-Service -DisplayName <System.String[]> [-Exclude <System.String[]>] [-Force] [-Include <System.String[]>]
    [-NoWait] [-PassThru] [-Confirm] [-WhatIf] [<CommonParameters>]

    Stop-Service [-InputObject] <System.ServiceProcess.ServiceController[]> [-Exclude <System.String[]>] [-Force]
    [-Include <System.String[]>] [-NoWait] [-PassThru] [-Confirm] [-WhatIf] [<CommonParameters>]

    Stop-Service [-Name] <System.String[]> [-Exclude <System.String[]>] [-Force] [-Include <System.String[]>]
    [-NoWait] [-PassThru] [-Confirm] [-WhatIf] [<CommonParameters>]
```

```
Stop-Service
[InputObject]<system.SerrviceProcess.ServiceController[]>
```

Means the cmdlet Stop-Service can accept one or more ServiceController
objects as input for the parameter -InputObject. Usually if you see a
parameter -InputObject it means that it will accept input from the pipeline
(see Pipeline section for more details).

Check the parameter can accept pipeline input using detailed help

Get-Help -Name Stop-Service -Full

```
-InputObject <System.ServiceProcess.ServiceController[]>
    Specifies ServiceController objects that represent the s
    objects, or type a command or expression that gets the o

    Required?                    true
    Position?                    0
    Default value                None
    Accept pipeline input?       True (ByValue)
    Accept wildcard characters?  false
```

So you can see ' Accept pipeline input? True' meaning you can pipe a ServiceController object to Stop-Service.

```
Get-Service -Name W32Time | Stop-Service
```

Properties

Properties are the attributes or data that is associated with an object. An object's properties can be queried by piping the object to Get-Member cmdlet with -Membertype parameter set to 'Property'.

```
Get-Service -Name W32Time | Get-Member -MemberType
Property
```

```
PS C:\> Get-Service -Name W32Time | Get-Member -MemberType Property


   TypeName: System.ServiceProcess.ServiceController

Name                MemberType Definition
----                ---------- ----------
CanPauseAndContinue Property   bool CanPauseAndContinue {get;}
CanShutdown         Property   bool CanShutdown {get;}
CanStop             Property   bool CanStop {get;}
Container           Property   System.ComponentModel.IContainer Container {get;}
DependentServices   Property   System.ServiceProcess.ServiceController[] DependentServices {get;}
DisplayName         Property   string DisplayName {get;set;}
MachineName         Property   string MachineName {get;set;}
ServiceHandle       Property   System.Runtime.InteropServices.SafeHandle ServiceHandle {get;}
ServiceName         Property   string ServiceName {get;set;}
ServicesDependedOn  Property   System.ServiceProcess.ServiceController[] ServicesDependedOn {get;}
ServiceType         Property   System.ServiceProcess.ServiceType ServiceType {get;}
Site                Property   System.ComponentModel.ISite Site {get;set;}
StartType           Property   System.ServiceProcess.ServiceStartMode StartType {get;}
Status              Property   System.ServiceProcess.ServiceControllerStatus Status {get;}
```

Returns all of the properties for the W32Time service. The Definition column also includes the verbs that can be used against each of the properties. So the DisplayName can amended using the Verb Set.

By default, not all properties are displayed when using the Get verb.

`Get-Service -Name W32Time` returns only three properties: -

```
PS C:\> Get-Service -Name W32Time

Status    Name           DisplayName
------    ----           -----------
Running   W32Time        Windows Time
```

To expand the display, you can pipe the output to Format-List (more about formatting later).

```
Get-Service -Name W32Time | Format-List
```

```
PS C:\> Get-Service -Name W32Time | Format-List


Name                  : W32Time
DisplayName           : Windows Time
Status                : Running
DependentServices     : {}
ServicesDependedOn    : {}
CanPauseAndContinue   : False
CanShutdown           : True
CanStop               : True
ServiceType           : Win32OwnProcess, Win32ShareProcess
```

But that still does not show all properties. Where is StartType?

Fortunately, we can select any property.

```
Get-Service -Name W32Time | Select-Object -Property Name,
Status, StartType
```

```
PS C:\> Get-Service -Name W32Time | Select-Object -Property Name, Status, StartType

Name     Status StartType
----     ------ ---------
W32Time Running    Manual
```

Most of your PowerShell scripts are going to read (Get) or write (Set) object properties in order to affect the systems that you are working on.

Methods

Methods are any actions that can be taken on an object.

To find the methods for any object, pipe the object to the Get-Member cmdlet and select the Methods. The screenshot below shows the method for the Process NotePad.

Remember to open Notepad before you try this command, or you will get an error - Cannot find a process with the name "notepad"

```
Get-Process -Name NotePad | Get-Member -MemberType Method
```

```
PS C:\> Get-Process -Name NotePad | Get-Member -MemberType Method


    TypeName: System.Diagnostics.Process

Name                      MemberType Definition
----                      ---------- ----------
BeginErrorReadLine        Method     void BeginErrorReadLine()
BeginOutputReadLine       Method     void BeginOutputReadLine()
CancelErrorRead           Method     void CancelErrorRead()
CancelOutputRead          Method     void CancelOutputRead()
Close                     Method     void Close()
CloseMainWindow           Method     bool CloseMainWindow()
CreateObjRef              Method     System.Runtime.Remoting.ObjRef CreateObjRef(type requestedType)
Dispose                   Method     void Dispose(), void IDisposable.Dispose()
Equals                    Method     bool Equals(System.Object obj)
GetHashCode               Method     int GetHashCode()
GetLifetimeService        Method     System.Object GetLifetimeService()
GetType                   Method     type GetType()
InitializeLifetimeService Method     System.Object InitializeLifetimeService()
Kill                      Method     void Kill()
Refresh                   Method     void Refresh()
Start                     Method     bool Start()
ToString                  Method     string ToString()
WaitForExit               Method     bool WaitForExit(int milliseconds), void WaitForExit()
WaitForInputIdle          Method     bool WaitForInputIdle(int milliseconds), bool WaitForInputIdle()
```

The Process NotePad has many methods including Kill. That means you can close the process by selecting the object and then invoking the Kill method (useful if NotePad were hanging for example)

```
$procToStop = Get-Process -Name NotePad
$procToStop.Kill()
```

Which can abbreviated to

```
(Get-Process -Name = NotePad).Kill()
```

The Pipeline

Many of the commands that you have used so far in this book have included the output of one command being piped to another using the vertical bar or pipe character (shift backslash on a US/UK QWERTY keyboard).

To get a list of process to find the ones that are using most CPU, we could a one liner like:

Get-Process | Sort-Object -Property CPU -Descending

If you look at the Object Type for Get-Process using the command

Get-Process | Get-Member you can see that it returns a collection of System.Diagnostics.Process objects that represent all of the processes running

The help for **Sort-Object – Get-Help -Name Sort-Object** shows that it accepts <System.Object> as input

SYNTAX
    Sort-Object [[-Property] <System.Object[]>] [-CaseSensitive] [-Culture <System.String>] [-Descending]
    [-InputObject
<System.Management.Automation.PSObject>] [-Unique]
[<CommonParameters>]

<System.Object> tells us that it accepts any object as input – so you can pipe just about anything to sort-object.

The pipe character instructs PowerShell to use the Output from the preceding command Get-Process to the command immediately following the pipe Sort-Object.

You can string multiple piped commands together e.g.

Get-Process | Select-Object -Property Processname, ID, CPU | Sort-Object -Property CPU -Descending

.Check your knowledge

✓ Find the Object Type for Installed Commands

✓ Display properties for a running process

✓ Open an application and kill its process

✓ using the Kill Method

✓ Get all Services and sort by status, then name using pipe

Pit Stop

Recap

Well done for getting this far, let us stop and review the progress you have made and recap and some important points.

By now you should be abel to:

Launch PowerShell

Create a simple script – on or more line commands

Format your script for readability

Save the script as a .ps1 file

Set the Execution Policy and run a saved script

These are the basic skills required to execute scripts that you download from the itnernet or that you write yourself.

In addition, you should also be abel to

Find commands

Get help for any gioven comand and understand the help syntax

Use parameters and switches

Understand the use of -WhatIf to check the effect of a command

Finally you should also be able to identify the module that commands are held in and install the module from PowerShell Gallery.

What's Next

Now that you understand the basics of PowerShell, we will go onto look at how to use remote management commands to manage remote machines, a common use case for Sys Admin use of PowerShell.

Then we will look at more advanced scripting techniques; variables, operators, loop etc and how to manage input and output.

Variables

Topics covered in this section

- Variable naming, types and scope
- Data types
- Assignment Operators

At the end of this section, you will be able to

- Define variables and update their values
- Explain how a variable scope affects its use
- Understand different variable types and common uses

Naming

A variable is a placeholder in memory that stores a value. The variable is represented by a dollar sign ($) followed by the variable name in camelCase.

Remember that PowerShell is not case sensitive by default so whilst you should use camelCase for your variable names, the upper- or lower-case name will reference the same variable so $varName is the same as $VARNAME and $varname. Try this out:

```
$varName = "PowerShell in insensitive"
If ($VARNAME -eq $varname) {
    Write-Host -Object "See they are all the same value"
    -BackgroundColor Red
} else {
    Write-Host "This author is not to be trusted"
}
```

By default, the variable name cannot contain a space or any character that is not alphanumeric or underscore. If you try to name a variable something like

$varBad!Name = "won't work" you will see an 'Unexpected token' error.

If you really have a need to name a variable like this – and to be clear you shouldn't - then you must enclose the variable name in braces

${varBad!Name} = "will work"
Remember to use the braces when referring to your variable in any subsequent operation.

Assignment Operators

In the examples above you have assigned a value to your variable using the equals (=) assignment operator. There are seven other operators that can be used when assigning a value to a variable.

Operator	Description
=	Sets the value of a variable to the specified value
+=	Increases the value of a variable by the specified value or appends the specified value to the existing value.
-=	Decreases the value of a variable by the specified value.
*=	Multiplies the value of a variable by the specified value or appends the specified value to the existing value.
/=	Divides the value of a variable by the specified value.
%=	Divides the value of a variable by the specified value and then assigns the remainder (modulus) to the variable.
++	Increases the value of a variable, assignable property, or array element by 1.
--	Decreases the value of a variable, assignable property, or array element by 1.

Table 4 Assignment Operators

These are for the most part intuitive. Where the operator can have multiple effects such as += the affect will depend on the data type. So,

```
$varNum = 0
$varNum += 5
$varNum
#     Will return the value 5
```
Whereas:

```
$varText = "Hello world"
$VarText += " I can write PowerShell"
$varText
# will return Hello world I can write PowerShell"
```

The operator ++ is shorthand for +=1 and is often used when counting or looping through an operation for a specified number of occurrences.

Data Type

As you can see in the example above, it is not strictly necessary to declare a data type to a variable as it will be set when creating the variable by assigning a value. This is referred to as being 'weakly typed'.

When writing your scripts, it is good practice to define the data type to make it easier for any future development work to understand what data type the variable was intended to hold and to avoids type mismatch errors.

Type mismatch errors occur when you try to assign a value or perform an operation that is the wrong data type. For example, the code:

```
$varText = "Hello World"
$varText ++
```

Returns a type mismatch error 'The '++' operator works only on numbers. The operand is a 'System.String''.

The data type is assigned in square brackets before the variable name on creation.

```
[String]$newVariable = "A text string"
```

This is then a 'strongly typed' variable. Strongly typed variables will prevent errors in your script and are also useful for ensuring that the intended data type support operators used later. Look at this example:

```
Write-Host -Object "Please Input a Number" -
backgroundColor Blue
#      Type 5 and press return
$varInput = Read-Host
$varInput += 10
$varInput
#      I bet you didn't expect that to output 510
```

$varInput | Get-Member will confirm that the data type was set to System.String when reading your input. So the operator += was interpreted as 'append the specified value to the existing value'.

Amend the script to set the variable to be strongly defined **[Int32]** **$varInput = Read-Host** and try again. This time the result is 15.

We will cover working with dates later, but dates are another good example where a strong typed variable can be essential. Look at this example:

```
$oldDate = "April 1, 1900"
$Today = Get-Date
$Days = ($Today - $oldDate).Days
Write-Host "$days have passed since April Fools 1900"
#      Will return an error as cannot subtract todays date
from a string
```

In order for this code snippet to work, you need to hard type the variable as a date using **[DateTime]$oldDate =   "April 1, 1900"**

Variables & Objects

So far, we have assigned explicit values to a variable, used assignment operators to derive a value and used Read-Host to accept user input.

The other big use case for variables that you need to be aware of is to hold an objects(s). Open a word document and run this:

```
$procToStop = Get-Process -Name WINWORD
$procToStop | Get-Member
```

You can see that the variable now has a type of System.Diagnostics.Process and supports all of the methods of a Process including Kill. Try it - Kill $procToStop using the Kill method.

Now imagine a script that finds all hung processes and kills them

```
$hungProc = Get-Process | Where-Object {$_.Responding -eq
$false}
Foreach ($procToKill in $hungProc){
    $procToKill.Kill()
}
```

Variables Scope
Variables can also have a scope that defines where they are available. When you type and run commands in a PowerShell session, you don't need to be aware of your variables' scope. When you move onto to more advanced activity like writing functions or calling scripts within scripts then it is useful to understand where your variables are available to be used.

PowerShell supports three scopes:

Global - is the scope that is available in any location. Variables that are created when PowerShell starts have the Global scope. e.g. Automatic Variables (more on those later).

Local – the current scope where the command is running that creates the variable. That could be in in a script, a function, or the Global context.

Script - the scope that is created when you run a script from a file.

Let's try to bring that to life with a simple example. The code below will create a variable in a function and then try to write the content of that variable outside of the function – the function will be covered in detail later, for now it is being used to demonstrate variable scope.

Cut and paste the following code into your session console:

```
Function scope {
    Param (
       [ Parameter () ]
        [String] $display
        )
    $messageText = "Hello World"
    If ($display) {
        Write-Host -Object " in the Script scope the
variable contains $messageText" -BackgroundColor Blue
    }
}
```

Then call the function with no parameters

Scope

and display the content of the variable $messageText as follows:

**Write-Host -Object "In the Local scope the variable
contains $messageText"   -Backgroundcolor red**

The message displayed in red background doesn't show the variable
$messageText "Hello World" as the variable is not available in the Local
scope. It is only available inside the function.

To prove that it is being set and can be displayed within the function, lets run
the function again but this time pass a parameter:

scope $true

this time you can see the variable is available within the function and it is
displayed in the massage.

Now let's amend your code to define the variable as global.

To do that we use the keyword 'global' - **$global:messageText**

```
Function scope {
    Param (
        [ Parameter () ]
        [String] $display
        )
    $global:messageText = "Hello World"
    If ($display) {
        Write-Host -Object " in the Script scope the
variable contains $global:messageText" -BackgroundColor
Blue
    }
}
```

Now if you call the function and use it to write to the screen, the global variable is available

```
scope
Write-Host -Object "In the Local scope the variable
contains $global:messageText"   -Backgroundcolor red
```

Private – private is not strictly speaking a scope. It is an option that restricts visibility of a variable outside of the scope where it is created.

Let's test that by defining two variables:

```
$varNoScope = "No explicit scope"
$private:varPrivateScope = "Private Scope"
```

Now we will try to use both of those variables within a simple function

```
Function scopetest {
    Write-Host -Object "The value of the un-scoped
variable is: $varNoScope"
-BackgroundColor Blue
    Write-Host -Object "The value of the private scoped
variable is: $private:varPrivateScope" -backgroundcolor
Red
}
scopetest
```

Here you can see the local scoped variable is available in the function whereas the private scoped variable is not. To prove no foul play and that the private variable contains a value

Write-Host "In the console the private variable value is: $varPrivateScope" -BackgroundColor Green

Types of Variables
There are threee major tyes of variables available in PowerShell.

User Created – these are the variabes that you create within your commands The variables do not persist, that is to say that they only exist while the PowerShell wibndow is open. When PowerShel is closed, the variables are deleted.

Automatic Variables – these are variables that store information about PowerShell. PowerShell creates them and manages their values. You cannot change the values of an automatic variable

Automatic Variable	Meaning
$$	Last token of the last line received by the shell.
$?	Success/fail status of the last operation.
$^	First token of the last line received by the shell.
$_	Current pipeline object in a pipelined script block.
$args	Array of parameters passed to the script, function, or script block.
$consoleFilename	Filename of the PowerShell console file that configured this session, if one was used.
$error	Array that holds the terminating and nonterminating errors generated in the shell.
$executionContext	Means by which scripts can access the APIs typically used by cmdlets and providers.
$false	Variable that represents the Boolean value False.
$foreach	Enumerator within a foreach loop.
$home	User's home directory.

Automatic Variable	Meaning
$host	Means by which scripts can access the APIs and implementation details of the current host and user interface.
$input	Current input pipeline in a pipelined script block.
$lastExitCode	Exit code of the last command. Can be explicitly set by scripts, and is automatically set when calling native executables.
$matches	Results of the last successful regular expression match (through the –match operator).
$myInvocation	Information about the context under which the script, function, or script block was run, including detailed information about the command (MyCommand) and the script that defines it (ScriptName).
$nestedPromptLevel	Nesting level of the current prompt. Incremented by operations that enter a nested prompt (such as $host.EnterNestedPrompt( )) and decremented by the exit statement.
$null	Variable that represents the concept of Null.
$pid	Process ID of the current PowerShell instance.
$profile	Location and filename of the PowerShell profile for this host.
$psHome	Installation location of PowerShell.
$PSItem	Same as $_ Current pipeline object in a pipelined script block.
$PSVersionTable	Contains a read-only hash table that displays details about the version of PowerShell that is running.
$shellId	Shell identifier of this host.
$stackTrace	Detailed stack trace information of the last error.
$this	Reference to the current object in ScriptMethods and ScriptProperties.
$true	Variable that represents the Boolean value True.

Many of these automatic variables are useful for debugging errors but there are a few other common uses including:

Setting bolean logic values true or false to a variable - **$varBoolean = $true** or **$varVoolean = $false**

Looking for null values - `if ($varempty = $null)`

Looping through the current pipleine object - `Get-Process | Foreach {$_.name}`

Check version of PowerShell installed - **$PSVersionTable.PSVersion**

Preference Variables – these are variables that store user preferences. Some hold default values but you can change the value of any preference variable.

You probably will not need to set any of these when you are first learngin to write brilliant PowerShell but they are added for completeness.

Preference Variable	Used for
$confirmPreference	Level of impact that operations may have before requesting confirmation. Supports the values none, low, medium, high. A value of none disables confirmation messages.
$debugPreference	How PowerShell should handle debug output written by a script or cmdlet. Supports the values SilentlyContinue, Continue, Inquire, and Stop.
$errorActionPreference	How PowerShell should handle error output written by a script or cmdlet. Supports the values SilentlyContinue, Continue, Inquire, and Stop.
$errorView	How PowerShell should output errors in the shell. Supports the values of Normal and CategoryView (a more

Preference Variable	Used for
	succinct and categorical view of the error).
$formatEnumerationLimit	Limit on how deep into an object the formatting and output facilities travel before outputting an object.
$InformationPreference	Sets information stream preferences that you want displayed to users. Takes one of the values: SilentlyContinue, Stop, Continue, Inquire, Ignore, Suspend, or Break.
$logCommandHealthEvent	Tells PowerShell to log command health events, such as errors and exceptions. Supports the values $true and $false.
$logCommandLifecycleEvent	Tells PowerShell to log command lifecycle events, such as Start and Stop. Supports the values $true and $false.
$logEngineHealthEvent	Tells PowerShell to log engine health events, such as errors and exceptions. Supports the values $true and $false.
$logEngineLifecycleEvent	Tells PowerShell to log engine lifecycle events, such as Start and Stop. Supports the values $true and $false.
$logProviderHealthEvent	Tells PowerShell to log provider health events, such as errors and exceptions. Supports the values $true and $false.
$logProviderLifecycleEvent	Tells PowerShell to log provider lifecycle events, such as Start and Stop. Supports the values $true and $false.
$MaximumHistoryCount	Determines how many commands are saved in the command history for the

Preference Variable	Used for
	current session.Valid values: 1 - 32768 (Int32)
$OFS	Specifies the character that separates the elements of an array that is converted to a string.
$OutputEncoding	Determines the character encoding method that PowerShell uses when it sends text to other applications.The valid values are as follows: Objects derived from an Encoding class, such as ASCIIEncoding, UTF7Encoding, UTF8Encoding, UTF32Encoding, and UnicodeEncoding.
$progressPreference	Controls how PowerShell should handle progress output written by a script or cmdlet. Supports the values SilentlyContinue, Continue, Inquire, and Stop.
$transcript	Filename used by the Start-Transcript cmdlet.
$verboseHelpErrors	Tells PowerShell to output detailed error information when parsing malformed help files. Supports the values $true and $false.
$verbosePreference	Controls how PowerShell should handle verbose output written by a script or cmdlet. Supports the values SilentlyContinue, Continue, Inquire, and Stop.
$warningPreference	Controls how PowerShell should handle warning output written by a script or cmdlet. Supports the

Preference Variable	Used for
	values SilentlyContinue, Continue, Inquire, and Stop.
$whatifPreference	Controls how PowerShell should handle confirmation requests called by a script or cmdlet. Supports the values SilentlyContinue, Continue, Inquire, and Stop.

Check your knowledge

 Can you determine what the output of the following command block would be?

```
[String]$varCalc = 5
$varCalc   += 10
$varCalc
```

 What is the value of the automatic variable $true set to when PowerShell is started?

 What operators could you use to increase the value of a numeric variable by 1?

 Can you explain the difference between a Global and Private variable Scope?

Operators

Operator Types

An operator is defined as one or more characters that determine the action to be taken on an object. PowerShell supports many different types of operators including:

Arithmetic Operators – Used to calculate values

Assignment Operators - Used to set, change or append values to variables

Comparison Operators – Used to compare values and test conditions

Logical Operators – Used to connect conditional statements into a single complex conditional

Other – there are other operator types supported used for redirection, for split and joins, and to find an object type.

Arithmetic Operators

Arithmetic operators are used to calculate numeric values. You can use one or more arithmetic operators to add, subtract, multiply, and divide values, and to calculate the remainder (modulus) of a division operation.

The addition operator (+) and multiplication operator (*) also operate on strings as described in the table below.

Operator	Description	Example
+	Adds numbers concatenates	6 + 4
	Concatenates strings	"Hello" + " " + "World"
-	Subtracts numbers	10 -8
	Reverses the numbers sign (negative to positive & vice versa)	- -10 - 10
*	Multiply numbers	5*3
	copy strings the specified number of time s	"Hello World " * 5
/	Divides two values	36/6
%	Returns the remainder of a division	13 % 3

In common with most arithmetic operations, they obey a strict order of precedence. So, 5 + 10 / 5 will return 7 not 3 as the division operator has a higher order of precedence than the addition operator.

From high to low the order or operator precedence in PowerShell is:

1. Parentheses ()
2. Unary or negative operator –
3. Multiplication and division */%
4. Addition and subtraction +-

Where there is more than one operator of the same precedence then they will be processed from left to right.

So, 6+9/3*2 returns 12 as the processing occurs in the following order

9/3 = 3
3*2 = 6
6+6 = 12

Parentheses can be used to change the order of processing:

(6+9)/3*2 returns 10

Rounding

By default, PowerShell will display numbers to the level of precision associated with the data type. So 11/3 will return 3.66666666666667

Does that make sense or are you still confused?

11/3 | Get-Member tells us that the result has TypeName: System.Double and referring back the tat data type table you can see that Double is a Double-precision 64-bit floating point number with 15-16 digits of precision.

There are a few commands that we can use to affect the level of precision returned. Let's stat by rounding to the nearest whole number. The simplest way is to define the result as an integer:

`[Int](11/3)` returns 4

You could also use the Round method from the Math class:

`[Math]::Round(11/3)`

The match class also supports allows you to set the precision. So, to return 2 decimal places use:

`[Math]::Round(11/3,2)`

You can also round up and down using the Ceiling and Floor methods:

`[Math]::Ceiling(11/3)`

`[Math]::Floor(11/3)`

One oddity that can catch out new user is that PowerShell rounds 0.5 to the nearest even integer. So:

`[Int](5/2) returns 2 (rounded down)`

but

`[Int](7/2) returns 4 (rounded up)`

If number precision and rounding are important to the processing in your script be as specific as you can using the Math functions.

Assignment Operators

Use assignment operators are used to assign, change, or append values to variables.

Operator	Description	Example
+=	Increases the value of a variable by the specified value or appends the specified value to the existing value.	$message = "Hello" $message +=" World"
-=	Decreases the value of a variable by the specified value.	$getToFive = 10 $getToFive -= 5
*=	Multiplies the value of a variable by the specified value or appends the specified value to the existing value.	$policeMan = "Hello " $policeMan * 3
/=	Divides the value of a variable by the specified value.	$getTo6 = 18 $getTo6 /3
%=	Divides the value of a variable by the specified value and then assigns the remainder (modulus) to the variable.	$leftOvers = 22 $leftOvers %=3
++	Increases the value of a variable, assignable property, or array element by 1.	$count = 0 $count ++
--	Decreases the value of a variable, assignable property, or array element by 1.	$countBack = 10 $countBack --

Table 5 - Assignment Operators

You can also combine arithmetic operators with assignment to assign the result of the arithmetic operation to a variable.

```
$baseNo = 3
$resultNo = $baseNo*3
$resultNo
```

Comparison Operators

Use comparison operators are used to compare values and test conditions. For example, you can compare two string values to determine whether they are equal.

Type	Operator	Comparison test
Equality	-eq	equals
	-ne	not equals
	-gt	greater than
	-ge	greater than or equal
	-lt	less than
	-le	less than or equal
Matching	-like	string matches wildcard pattern
	-notlike	string does not match wildcard pattern
	-match	string matches regex pattern
	-notmatch	string does not match regex pattern
Replacement	-replace	replaces strings matching a regex pattern
Containment	-contains	collection contains a value
	-notcontains	collection does not contain a value
	-in	value is in a collection
	-notin	value is not in a collection
Type	-is	both objects are the same type
	-isnot	the objects are not the same type

Table 6 - Comparison Operators

By default, all string comparison operators are not case sensitive, so

"NOT CASE MATCHED" -eq "not case matched" returns true.

To force case sensitivity, prefix the operator with a c (for case) after the dash

"CASE MATCHED" -ceq "case matched" returns false

Equality operators will return Boolean True or False depending on how the values either side of the operator compare, and the operator used.

Matching Operators find elements that match or don't match the specified pattern. When the input to the operator is a single value, the operator will return Boolean True or False. If the input is a collection of values, then the matching values will be returned.

Matching operators support the use of wildcards. The most powerful Wildcard is the asterisk * that means match one or more of any character. Hence

"Hello World" -like "*world" returns true

"Goodbye World" -like "*world" returns true

"Hello World" –like "world" returns false when no wildcard is used as a literal match is required.

Remembering that the operator is not case sensitive. Another useful wildcard supported is:

? - Matches one character in that position. So, the following will all return True.

"mat" -like "?at"
"rat" -like "?at"
"sat" -like "?at"

But these are all False

"brat" -like "?at"
"spat" -like "?at"
"mate" -like "?at"

As mentioned earlier, If the input is a collection of values, then the matching values will be returned. The code below returns 'mouse and 'house'

$arrayValues =@("mouse", "house", "moose", "hose")

$arrayValues -like "?ouse"

-notlike is the inverse of -like and looks for the absence of a match

```
$arrayValues =@("mouse", "house", "moose", "hose")
```

```
$arrayValues -notlike "?ouse"
```

Returns 'moose' and 'hose'

Equality operators -match and -notmatch will match a string using regex or regular expressions. See the section below on Regex for more details on how to write regular expressions.

Replacement Operators also uses regular expressions to find the specified pattern and then replaces the matches with the specified replacement value.

A simple example might look like:

```
"Hello World" -replace "ld", "ms"
```

Were you expecting that output returned?

A more useful example might be to rename all files in a folder that end in .txt to be .log files

```
Get-ChildItem *.txt | Rename-Item -NewName { $_.name -replace '\.txt$','.log' }
```

Containment Operators are like equality operators, except they always return a Boolean value, even when the input is a collection. They also stop comparing as soon as a match is found. In a very large collection, they return quicker than the equality operators. So the following code returns True

```
$varArray = @("red", "blue","green","yellow", "red")
$varArray -contains "red"
```

As would

```
"red" -in $varArray
```

But not

```
"green" -notin $varArray
```

Type Operators are used to determine if an object is a specific type.

As we have seen, some operators behave differently depending on the object type they are applied to, so there may be scenarios where you want to check the object is of a specified type

Look at the example below

```
[Int]$variableA = 5
[String]$variableB = 5
```

$variableA ***2** returns 10 whereas **$variableB** ***2** returns 55. To check if the variable is an integer, we can use the -is type operator.

$variableB -is [Int] returns False whereas

$variableA -is [Int] returns True

Logical Operators
Logical Operators connect expressions and statements, allowing you to use a single expression to test for multiple conditions.

Operator	Description	Example
-and	Logical AND. Returns true only when both statements are true	(1 -eq 1) -and (1 -eq 2) False
-or	Logical OR. Returns true when either statement is true	(1 -eq 1) -or (1 -eq 2) True
-xor	Logical EXCLUSIVE OR. Returns true when only one statement is TRUE	(1 -eq 1) -xor (2 -eq 2) False
-not	Logical not. Negates the statement that follows.	-not (1 -eq 1) False
!	Same as -not	!(1 -eq 1)

Table 7- Logical Operators

Logical operators are incredibly useful to connect statements to build complex comparison statements. You will cover If Then Else loops in the next chapter, but they are a great example of where you can connect operators.

Statements that use logical operators always return a Boolean True or False value. That is why they are often used in an If statement.

```
$varArray = @("red", "blue","green","yellow", "red")
$varArray -contains "red"
If ($varArray -contains "red" -and $varArray -contains
"yellow"){
    Write-Host -Object "There are red and yellow in your
array"
}
```

The operator for logical not **-not** is more often expressed in the sort form of an exclamation mark so the command. So:

```
-not ("red" -in $varArray)
```
Is the same as

```
!("red" -in $varArray)
```
Which happens to be the same as

```
"red" -notin $varArray
```

You will see that there are often multiple ways to get the same results and you will develop your own scripting style overtime.

Check your knowledge

 What operators can you use to check if two values are different?

 What does the * operator do when used on a String?

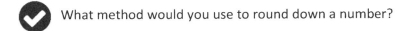 What method would you use to round down a number?

What operator is ! equal to?

What result would the following code return?

```
$inputVar = "10*5"
$inputVar -is [int]
```

Loops

Loops

Once you start to write PowerShell scripts, you are likely to come across scenarios where you want your code to loop through a series of commands. That might be to loop through a list of servers, reading rows from an external file or just reiterating code a specified number of times.

PowerShell supports a variety of loops. Whilst they all vary in the specification of the condition, they all follow the same general pattern

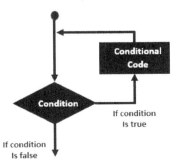

79

For Loop

PowerShell's for loop executes a sequence of commands multiple times and abbreviates the code that manages the loop. The loop consists of a for statement defining the initial counter value (usually 0), the condition which if true executes the code and the code to increment the counter. The command block to execute whilst the condition is true is wrapped in braces {}. The condition is evaluated every time the loop runs and if true it will execute the code block again.

for (<Initial counter value>; (<Condition>; <Code to increment counter>)
{
   <Code Block>
}

So, to loop though a command block ten times, your code could look like this:

```
For ($count=0; $count -lt 10; $count++)
{
    Write-host -Object "Counter is set to $count"
}
```

Remember the operator ++ increments the variable $counter by 1 and the code repeats whilst the value of $counter is less than 10 (0 to 9 = 10 times).

Omitting the values for the counter, condition and incrementor would create a never ending loop.

```
For (;;)
{
    Write-Host -Object "Still Counting $counter"
    $counter++
}
```

(Use Ctrl>C to break out of the loop if your code gets stuck in a never-ending loop).

Multiple operations are allowed for in the For statement, each is enclosed in parentheses and separated by a comma.

As an example, the following code sets both the $counter variable to 0 and also initialises a variable $fgcolor to Blue. When the $counter variable is incremented to advance the loop, the variable $fgcolor is also changed (to a random value from $colors array).

```
$colors =
@("Green","Cyan","Red","Magenta","Yellow","White")
for (($counter=0),($fgcolor = "Blue") ;$counter -lt 10;
($counter ++), ($fgcolor = $colors | Get-Random)) {
    Write-Host -Object  "counting  $counter" -
ForegroundColor $fgcolor
}
```

If you want to get creative with your For loop, you can simply add a progress bar using the PowerShell utility Write-Progress

```
For ($counter=0; $counter -lt 100; $counter++) {
    Sleep 1
    Write-Progress -Activity "Progress" -Status
"$counter% Complete:"                         -
PercentComplete $counter;
}
```

To find out more about Write-progress use: Help Write-progress -online

For Each Loop

PowerShell's For Each loop is used to step through a series of values in a collection, executing code for each value found.

It is often used to work on values held in an array or to loop through a collection of objects returned by a query. The loop consists of a ForEach statement which defines a variable to hold each object and the collection to step through. The command block to execute whilst stepping through the collection is wrapped in braces {}.

```
foreach (<item> in <collection>)
{
<Code Block>
}
```

To step through a collection inside an array your code would look like

```
$colors =
@("Green","Cyan","Red","Magenta","Yellow","White")
Foreach($fgcolor in $colors){
    Write-host -Object "The text is now $fgcolor" -
ForegroundColor $fgcolor
}
```

To step though the results of a command we can either store the results in a variable and then use the variable in the foreach command like this:

```
$results = Get-Service
Foreach ($service in $results){
    $message = "Found the service " + $service.name
    $message += " with the status " + $service.status
    Write-Host -Object $message
}
```

Or alternately pipe the get verb command directly to the loop using ForEach-Object:

```
Get-Service | ForEach-Object{$message =  "Found "+
$_.name + " with status "+ $_.status; Write-Host -Object
$message}
```

Also note that the ForEach-Object has an alias of % (percentage sign). When looking at scripts found on the internet you will often see it used for brevity thus:

```
Get-Service | %{$message =  "Found "+ $_.name + " with
status "+ $_.status; Write-Host -Object $message}
```

You will also have noticed that the automatic variable "$_" is being used to reference the current pipeline object.

While Loops
The while loop evaluates a statement first and if true will execute the specified command block. The while statement contains the condition to evaluate and the command block wrapped in braces {}. The condition is evaluated first and the code block only runs if the condition is true.

while (<Condition>) {
<Code Block>
}
You will notice that there is no code in the while statement to set or control any object referenced in the condition. You must manage it within the code block (to prevent a never-ending loop).

```
$counter = 0
while ($counter -lt 10) {
    Write-Host "I am still counting - $counter"
    $counter ++
}
```

In the above example, the command $counter ++ advances the loop counter within the code block.

Do-While Loops
A do-while loop is a variety of the while loop. The do-while statement consists of a block of commands followed by the condition to evaluate. The condition is evaluated after the script block has run. As in a While loop, the script block is repeated if the condition evaluates to true.

do {
  <Code Block>
} while (<Condition>)

As the condition is evaluated after the code has run, it will always run once regardless of the state of the condition. Like a While loop, code to affect the condition must be contained within the code block.

```
$counter =0
do {
    Write-Host -Object "how many times will this line get
written - $counter"
    $counter ++
} while ($counter -lt 0)
```

Once the condition returns False, the loop exits and control moves back to the parent code block.

```
$counter = 0
do {
    Write-Host -Object "The current value is $counter" -
ForegroundColor Blue
    $counter ++;
} while ($counter -lt 10)
Write-Host -Object "now running code outside the loop" -
ForegroundColor Green
```

Do-Until Loops

Do-Until loops are the reverse of Do-While in that the code executes only until the condition becomes true. The command construct is similar to do-while.

```
do {
  <Code Block>
} while (<Condition>)
```

Like a While loop, code to affect the condition must be contained within the code block.

Seer the example on the next page:

```
$counter =0
do {
    Write-Host -Object "how many times will this line get
written - $counter"
    $counter ++
} until ($counter -ge 10)
```

If Then Else Conditional Statement

PowerShell has statements that allow you to execute code conditionally. The If statement evaluates the condition and id true will run the code block wrapped in braces {}.

```
if (<Condition>) {
   <Code Block>
   }
```

If the condition returns false then the cod block is skipped.

```
$value = "cat"
$pets = "cat", "dog", "gerbil", "hamster"
if ($value -in $pets) {
    Write-Host -Object "$value is a pet"
}
```

Now set $value = "Monkey" and try that script again.

You can optionally add an alternate execution path by appending Else:

```
if (<Condition>) {
<Code Block
} Else {
<Alternate Code Block>
}
```

So, updating the code above:

```
$value = "monkey"
$pets = "cat", "dog", "gerbil", "hamster"
```

```
if ($value -in $pets) {
    Write-Host -Object "$value is a pet"
} Else {
    Write-Host -Object "$value is not a pet"
}
```

The alternate execution path can also be made to be conditional using Else If. Multiple Else-If statements can be combined:

```
$value = "Dinosaur"
$pets = "cat", "dog", "gerbil", "hamster"
if ($value -in $pets) {
    Write-Host -Object "$value is a pet"
} `
elseif ($value -eq "monkey") {
    Write-Host -Object "$value is not a pet"
}`
elseif ($value -notin $pets) {
    Write-Host -Object "I don't know what $value is"
}
```

Note that the elseif statement needs to follow immediately after the If statement or it will return an error 'The term 'elseif' is not recognized as the name of a cmdlet, function, script file, or operable program'. Hence the use of backticks above (which are not good as discussed earlier).

If creating a long list of if-else statements, you should look at using Switch instead.

Switch Statement

The switch statement allows you to provide a variable and a list of possible values. If the value matches the variable, then its code block is executed. It is useful when comparing an object to a list of different possible values that's is too long to be managed in an if-then-elseif block.

```
switch(<test-value>) {
  <condition> {<action>}
  <condition> {<action>}
  <condition> {<action>}
}
```

```
$value =  "Unicorn"
Switch ($value){
Dog { Write-Host -Object "$value is a pet"}
Cat { Write-Host -Object "$value is a pet"}
Monkey { Write-Host -Object "$value is a wild animal"}
Dinosaur { Write-Host -Object "$value is extinct"}
Unicorn { Write-Host -Object "$value is a mythical
creature"}
Santa { Write-Host -Object "$value is real"}
}
```

Remember that by default switch is not case sensitive so monkey, Monkey and MONKEY will all match case 2 above (start counting from zero). Also note that if your value matches more than one case, all cases that match will be executed.

If you pass an array to the switch statement, it will process each value in the array

```
$value =  "Unicorn","Dog","dinosaur","SANTA"
Switch ($value){
Dog { Write-Host -Object "$_ value is a pet"}
Cat { Write-Host -Object "$_ is a pet"}
Monkey { Write-Host -Object "$_ is a wild animal"}
Dinosaur { Write-Host -Object "$_ is extinct"}
Unicorn { Write-Host -Object "$_ is a mythical creature"}
Santa { Write-Host -Object "$_ is real"}
}
```

Nesting Loops

Loops can be nested, that's is to say that you can have a loop contained within the code block for another loop. Let's create a ForEach loop that has a conditional If Then Else loop nested within it:

```
foreach (<item> in <collection>)
{
  if (<Condition>) {
    <Code Block
  } Else {
  <Alternate Code Block>
  }
}
```

We will re-use our pet checker code again in the next example:

```
$values = "cat", "gerbil", "monkey", "dog", "dinosaur"
$pets = "cat", "dog", "gerbil", "hamster"
foreach( $animal in $values) {
    if ($animal -in $pets) {
        Write-Host -Object "$animal is a pet"
    } Else {
        Write-Host -Object "$animal is not a pet"
    }
}
```

Whilst the maximum depth of nested groups in PowerShell is far beyond what you are going to need, deep nested groups are not performant and are also hard to write and maintain properly.

Take a look at the next example that recursively enumerates AD groups

```
        [string]$Group,
        [int]$Depth = 0
        Get-ADGroupMember -Identity $Group | ForEach-
Object {
        If ($_.objectClass -eq "Group")
        {
            If ($Script:Groups.ContainsKey($_.Name))
            {
                [PSCustomObject]@{
                    Name            = $_.Name
                    SamAccountName = $_.SamAccountName
                    Group           = $Group
                    Depth           = $Depth
                    CircularGroup  = $true
                }
            }
            Else
            {
                $Script:Groups.Add($_.Name,$true)
                GetGroupRecurse -Group $_.Name -Depth
($Depth + 1)
            }
        }
        Else
        {
            [PSCustomObject]@{
                Name            = $_.Name
                SamAccountName = $_.SamAccountName
                Group           = $Group
                Depth           = $Depth
                CircularGroup  = $false
            }
        }
    }
}
```

Multiple levels of nesting make it hard to understand where each command is in the hierarchy of the nest.

You can avoid deep nesting by breaking out commands into Functions (covered later)

Break and Continue
The break statement provides a way to exit the current loop. It can be used to exit a ForEach, For, While, Do-While, Do-Until or a Switch loop. When a break statement is executed, control moves to the next line of code outside of the block.

It can be useful to break out of a loop if an unexpected value is encountered. For example, in the snippet below, the loop counts backwards from 10 and stops at 5.

```
$varStart = 10
Do {
    "Starting the loop $varStart"
    $varStart -= 1
    Start-Sleep -seconds 1
 } While ($varStart -ge 5)
```

But change the starting value of $varStart to 4 and it still executes the code block one time. To stop that you can add a check and break the loop if the initial value is set (using a nested if-then loop):

```
$varStart = 10
Do {
    If ($varStart -lt 5) {
        Break
    }
    "Starting the loop $varStart"
    $varStart -= 1
    Start-Sleep -seconds 1
 } While ($varStart -ge 5)
Write-Host -Object "The loop has ended"
```

Remember that the break command is used to exit the current loop. When you have nested loops, it will break the loop that it is enclosed within. For example:

```
$loopOne = 1
$loopTwo  = 1
While($loopOne -le 10 ){
    Write-Host —Object "Loop One Count is $loopOne" -
ForegroundColor Green
    while($loopTwo -le 5 ){
                Write-Host -Object "Loop Two Count is
$loopTwo" -ForegroundColor Blue
        $loopTwo ++
    }
     $loopTwo  = 1
     if($loopOne -eq 5){Break}
     $loopOne++
     Start-Sleep -milliseconds 500
}
Write-Host -Object "The value of Loop 1 is $loopOne and
Loop 2 is $loopTwo" -BackgroundColor Red
```

A simple counting script that used two nested loops to count from 1 to 5, ten times. Except the outer loop (loop One) has a break statement when it reaches 5.

As the break is contained in the outer loop, the inner loops also ends and control moves to the next block of code outside of loop one - Write-Host -Object "The value of Loop 1 is $loopOne and Loop 2 is $loopTwo" - BackgroundColor Red

Conversely you could break the inner loop and allow the outer loop to continue like this:

```
$loopOne = 1
$loopTwo  = 1
While($loopOne -le 10 ){
    Write-Host —Object "Loop One Count is $loopOne" -
ForegroundColor Green
    while($loopTwo -le 5 ){
                Write-Host -Object "Loop Two Count is
$loopTwo" -ForegroundColor Blue
        $loopTwo ++
            if($loopTwo -eq 4){Break}
    }
```

```
    $loopTwo  = 1
    $loopOne++
   Start-Sleep -milliseconds 500
}
Write-Host -Object "The value of Loop 1 is $loopOne and
Loop 2 is $loopTwo" -BackgroundColor Red
```

This time the If-Then statement will break the inner loop (loop two) when it gets to 3 but allow the outer loop (loop one) to count to ten.

The Continue statement exits the current instance of a loop and returns control to the top of the loop. This means that the current loop stops running any further commands but continues execution, rather than exiting completely.

Take a look at this simple script. We will loop from one to 10 but if the counter number is even, we will continue to the top of the loop.

```
for ($count=1; $count -le 10; $count++)
{
if ($count%2 -eq 0) {
    continue}
    Write-host -Object "Counter is set to $count"
}
```

We used the modulo operator to check that the number was even (remainder = 0 when divided by 2) and then called the Continue statement to move back to the top of the loop and continue.

Can you think of more instances where you can use the continue statement such as to loop through a list of servers and ignore any not responding to ping?

```
Foreach($remoteComputer in $serverList){
   if (Test-Connection -BufferSize 32 -Count 1 -ComputerName
   $remoteComputer -Quiet) {
       Continue
   }
   # do something
}
```

Look – you are using nested loops, operators and the continue statement in a simple script.

Check your knowledge

How could you loop through an array of objects?

Can you explain the difference between Do-While and Do-Until?

Is the Else statement option in an If-Then-Else loop?

When would you use a switch statement?

How do you break out of a nested loop and end both loops?

What command would you use to move control from an inner loop to an outer loop?

How many times would code inside this loop be executed

```
For ( $a=0, $a -le 10, $a++) { <<code>>}
```

Input

Topics covered in this section

- Get contents of a file
- Reading User Input

At the end of this section, you will be able to

- Open a file and read its content as input

So now that you are starting to write more advanced scripts with loops and conditional statements, it is logical that you might want to fetch data to use in your script that is not held in a .net object.

Firstly, let's look at how your script can get input from the user.

Read Host

You can prompt for user input in PowerShell by using the Read-Host cmdlet. The Read-Host cmdlet reads a line of input from the PowerShell console. Get-Help Read-Host shows the following syntax:

```
Read-Host [[-Prompt] <System.Object>] [-AsSecureString]
[<CommonParameters>]
```

-Prompt is an optional parameter that specifies the text prompt to be displayed

-AsSecureString is a switch that will replace the characters typed with asterisks (*) on screen and holds the value as a Secure String.

Note that the cmdlet also accepts common parameters (see earlier section on Common Parameters).

Of course, you will usually want to capture the input in a variable to use later. In the following example we will ask for a name and then use it to search Active Directory and returns the users logon name.

```
$userInput = Read-Host -Prompt "Name to search for"
$ADUser = Get-ADUser -Filter {Name -Like $userInput}
$accountName= $ADUser.SamAccountName
Write-Host "$userInput has an AD account $AccountName"
```

Note that this simple script has no error handling and if the user does not exist in AD it will return a null logon name. Read the action Error Handling and then come back and update the script to better manage a non-existent user.

You should also take care when prompting a user for input as you might not get back the data type that you expect. Look at this simple example to ask for a number, calculate its squared value it and return the result:

```
$baseNo = Read-Host -Prompt "Give me a number to square"
$squareNo = $baseNo * $baseNo
Write-Host "$baseNo squared is $squareNo"
```

Now input 3 and ... hold on by my math 3^2 should equal 9 not 333. The difference in result that you see is because the input has been interpreted by PowerShell as a string (remember you can check that either using the method **$baseno.gettype()** or by piping the variable to **Get-Member** cmdlet).

Try again but this time lets specify that we want the input to be a number

```
[int32]$baseNo = Read-Host -Prompt "Give me a number to square"
$squareNo = $baseNo * $baseNo
Write-Host "$baseNo squared is $squareNo"
```

In this example you have specified that the variable $baseNo is a number (32bit integer). This technique is known as type casting. You still need to be careful, run the script again but this time type the word 'three' at the prompt. Did you see the error ' Cannot convert value "three" to type "System.Int32". Error: "Input string was not in a correct format." '

Twenty-five years in IT has taught me that users do funny things so always be careful when reading user input. Always validate, check the data type, look for special characters, check numbers are wildly out of bounds, encode anything that will be used to form a SQL statement etc.

Also take care when using the -AsSecureString switch as it will limit what can be done with the output. Look how few methods are supported.

Name	MemberType	Definition
AppendChar	Method	void AppendChar(char c)
Clear	Method	void Clear()
Copy	Method	securestring Copy()
Dispose	Method	void Dispose(), void IDisposable.Dispose()
Equals	Method	bool Equals(System.Object obj)
GetHashCode	Method	int GetHashCode()
GetType	Method	type GetType()
InsertAt	Method	void InsertAt(int index, char c)
IsReadOnly	Method	bool IsReadOnly()
MakeReadOnly	Method	void MakeReadOnly()
RemoveAt	Method	void RemoveAt(int index)
SetAt	Method	void SetAt(int index, char c)
ToString	Method	string ToString()
Length	Property	int Length {get;}

If you want to get a masked username/password look to use Get-Credential instead.

Get-Content

As well as getting input from the user, you might need to read and use the contents of a file. The simplest way to extract data from a file is probably with the Get-File cmdlet

```
Get-Content -Path <<path.filename>>
```

Remember to use the full file path name as the shortcut .\ points to the current folder where the script is being run.

To test the cmdlet, create a simple text file using the following command:

```
1..10 | ForEach-Object { Add-Content -Path
.\PSSampleFile.txt -Value "This is line $_" }
```

Now you can read the content of this text file into an array

```
$fileContent = Get-Content -Path .\PSSampleFile.txt
```

And then loop through the new array to display each line

```
$lineNo = 1
$fileContent | ForEach-Object {Write-Host -Object "Line
$lineNo  contains $_"; $lineNo ++}
```

So, imagine that you had a list of leavers' logon names in a file called leavers.csv, you could read the file, loop through and remove the users from AD very quickly:

```
$leavers = Get-Content -Path u:\leavers.csv | ForEach-
Object { Remove-ADUser -Identity $_ -Confirm}
```

Please don't use this in a production environment, this is a simple example and I have left the -confirm switch in there just in case. You would probably want to build a match more elegant script with error handling and checks to ensure that you are not deleting all users by mistake. You might also want to check that the AD account is disabled before it gets deleted.

Import-CSV

Get-Contents will work fine if you want to read a csv field and have each line as a single value, but it is more likely that you want a multi-dimensional array (or hashtable - more on those later) where each row is broken down into the comma delimiters value and each value held as a separate referenceable item.

So, if I were to create a comma-separated file that 6 lines looking like this:

First,Last,email,dept
John,Smith,john.smith@domain.com,HR Dept
Anne,Brown,anne.browne@domain.com,Finance
Wendy,Jones,wendy.jones@domain.com,Legal
Bob,Bobson,bob.bobson@domain.com,Legal
Lesley,Black,lesely.black@domain.com,IT Support

and saved it as c:\temp\users.csv – when you use Get-Contents to read the file

```
$userDetails = Get-Content -Path C:\temp\users.csv
```

You can see that the resulting variable holds one entry for each line of the file

Now try

```
$userDetails = Import-CSV -Path C:\temp\users.csv
```

In this example, the cmdlet Import-CSV creates a custom object that looks more like a table (it is an associative array or hashtable).

First	Last	Email	Dept
John	Smith	john.smith@domain.com	HR Dept
Anne	Brown	anne.browne@domain.com	Finance
Wendy	Jones	wendy.jones@domain.com	Legal
Bob	Bobson	bob.bobson@domain.com	Legal
Lesley	Black	lesely.black@domain.com	IT Support

We will cover how to reference each field in more detail in the section on arrays. Here are a few things to try in the meanwhile:

```
$userDetails | foreach-object {
$fullname = $_.first + " " + $_.last
$email = $_.Email
Write-Host -Object "the email address for $fullname is
$Email"
}
```

Or

```
$msg = ($userDetails | where dept -eq "Legal").count
Write-Host " There are $msg people in Legal"
```

Import-Excel

You have seen that Get-Content and Import-CSV can be used to read simple text files such as .txt and .csv comma separated files.

More advanced methods to read excel spreadsheets are not covered in this publication but you might want to check out the module ImportExcel which can be installed (with admin privileges) using the install-module cmdlet.

```
Install-Module ImportExcel
```

Within this fantastic module created by the very talented Doug Finke you will find cmdlets like Import-Excel that read the contents of an excel file as simply as

```
$stores = Import-Excel C:\Temp\store.xlsx
```

Of course, you could just open the excel spreadsheet and save it as a .CSV file.

Check your knowledge

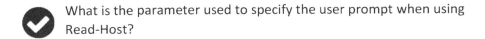 What is the parameter used to specify the user prompt when using Read-Host?

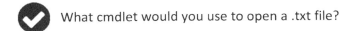 What cmdlet would you use to open a .txt file?

 What is type casting and why might you use it?

What is the difference between Get-Content and Import-CSV when opening a comma separated file?

Output

> Topics covered in this section
>
> - Formatting Output
> - Output to a file
>
>   At the end of this section, you will be able to
>
> - Display output as a table
> - Control the length of output
> - Save output to a file

As you begin to write more PowerShell and present more data to the screen, it won't be long until you see the dreaded PowerShell ellipses (...)

```
PS C:\> get-service -Name B*_

Status     Name                 DisplayName
------     ----                 -----------
Stopped    BcastDVRUserSer...   GameDVR and Broadcast User Service_...
Running    BDESVC               BitLocker Drive Encryption Service
Running    BFE                  Base Filtering Engine
Stopped    BITS                 Background Intelligent Transfer Ser...
Running    BluetoothUserSe...   Bluetooth User Support Service_11329d
Running    bomgar-ps-60C85...   BeyondTrust Remote Support Jump Cli...
Running    BrokerInfrastru...   Background Tasks Infrastructure Ser...
Stopped    Browser              Computer Browser
Running    BTAGService          Bluetooth Audio Gateway Service
Running    BthAvctpSvc          AVCTP service
Running    bthserv              Bluetooth Support Service
```

This is default behaviour of PowerShell as it does not calculate the required size of any column (actually it uses a default width value but more on that later). The ellipsis or three dots (...) indicate that the field has been truncated.

103

Fortunately, PowerShell has a number of commands to help with formatting. Find them with the command Get-Command -Verb Format

Format-Table -AutoSize

The quickest way to get around the ellipsis is to try piping your output to the the Format-Table cmdlet. Here are the results again from my laptop when I execute

Get-Service -Name B*| Format-Table -AutoSize

```
PS C:\> get-service -Name B*|Format-Table -AutoSize

Status   Name                              DisplayName
------   ----                              -----------
Stopped  BcastDVRUserService_11329d        GameDVR and Broadcast User Service_11329d
Running  BDESVC                            BitLocker Drive Encryption Service
Running  BFE                               Base Filtering Engine
Stopped  BITS                              Background Intelligent Transfer Service
Running  BluetoothUserService_11329d       Bluetooth User Support Service_11329d
Running  bomgar-ps-60CB54A3-1634562724     BeyondTrust Remote Support Jump Client [rsagroup.beyondtrustcloud.com]
Running  BrokerInfrastructure              Background Tasks Infrastructure Service
Stopped  Browser                           Computer Browser
Running  BTAGService                       Bluetooth Audio Gateway Service
Running  BthAvctpSvc                       AVCTP service
Running  bthserv                           Bluetooth Support Service
```

Use Get-Help for more details on how to use Format-Table. Notice that it has a parameter -InputObject so I could have run

Format-Table -InputObject (Get-Service -Name B*) - Autosize

Enclosing the Get-Service cmdlet in brackets references its output as an object. Without the brackets this command would fail. The more PowerShell you write and view online, you will see that here are often many different ways to achieve the same outcome and preference, style and memory of commands will play a part on how you shape your scripts.

The Format-Table cmdlet might still truncate data, but it only truncates at the end of the screen. Properties, other than the last one displayed, are given as much size as they need for their longest data element to display correctly.

```
PS C:\> Get-Service -Name B* |Format-table -property Name, RequiredServices, CanShutDown, CanStop, DisplayName -Autosize

Name                              RequiredServices                     CanShutdown CanStop DisplayName
----                              ----------------                     ----------- ------- -----------
BcastDVRUserService_11329d        {}                                         False   False GameDVR and Broadcast User Servi...
BDESVC                            {}                                         False    True BitLocker Drive Encryption Service
BFE                               {RpcSs}                                    False    True Base Filtering Engine
BITS                              {RpcSs}                                    False   False Background Intelligent Transfer ...
BluetoothUserService_11329d       {}                                         False    True Bluetooth User Support Service_1...
bomgar-ps-60C854A3-1634562724     {}                                          True    True BeyondTrust Remote Support Jump ...
BrokerInfrastructure              {DcomLaunch, RpcSs, RpcEptMapper}          False   False Background Tasks Infrastructure ...
Browser                           {LanmanServer, LanmanWorkstation}          False   False Computer Browser
BTAGService                       {rpcss}                                    False    True Bluetooth Audio Gateway Service
BthAvctpSvc                       {rpcss}                                    False    True AVCTP service
bthserv                           {}                                          True    True Bluetooth Support Service
```

Of course, you can use the -Property parameter to change the order of the fields if you have a preference as to what is truncated and what isn't.

Format Table -Wrap

If you are still concerned with the end fields being truncated, you can use the -Wrap switch to word-wrap any fields that do not fit the screen.

Try

```
Get-Service -Name B* |Format-Table -Property Name,
RequiredServices, CanShutDown, CanStop, DisplayName -
Autosize -Wrap
```

Ignore, for now, the RequiredServices and look at how the DisplayName is wrapped across the line where it is too long to fit the screen.

Format-List

If the table still can't fit all the fields you want to see on screen, try Format-List. Format-List will display the object as a list with each field labelled. So,

```
Get-Service -Name B*|Format-List
```

would look like this:

105

```
PS C:\> Get-Service -Name B*|Format-List


Name                  : BcastDVRUserService_13759fb
DisplayName           : GameDVR and Broadcast User Service_13759fb
Status                : Stopped
DependentServices     : {}
ServicesDependedOn    : {}
CanPauseAndContinue   : False
CanShutdown           : False
CanStop               : False
ServiceType           : 224
```

Look at the parameters for Format-List. You can use the -Property parameter to specify the fields to be displayed and the order tin which to display them.

Get-Service -Name B*|Format-List -Property Name, DisplayName, CanStop, Status

```
PS C:\> Get-Service -Name B*|Format-List -Property Name, DisplayName, CanStop, Status


Name        : BcastDVRUserService_13759fb
DisplayName : GameDVR and Broadcast User Service_13759fb
CanStop     : False
Status      : Stopped
```

Out-GridView

The Out-GridView cmdlet sends the output from a command to a new grid view window where the output is displayed in an interactive table.

Try it

Get-Process | Out-GridView

The table allows you to

- Hide, Show, and Reorder Columns
- Sort rows
- Quick Filter
- Add Criteria Filter
- Copy and paste

Redirection Operators

OK So the output looks great on screen, but what if you want to save it to a file. Well, fortunately PowerShell supports various methods and cmdlets to do that.

Let's start with the simplest, the redirection operators > and >>

> 	Sends the specified stream to a file

>> 	Appends the specified stream to a file

You will no doubt have noticed that the description talks about a specified stream. For simply saving the results of a series of commands to a file you can ignore that for now.

```
Get-Process | Sort-Object -Property CPU -Descending >
C:\temp\process.txt
```

The example above redirects the output from a file to a txt file. Be careful, if the file already exists it will be overwritten without any warning.

Changing to a double chevron means that the content is appended to the end of the file.

```
Get-Service >> C:\temp\process.txt
```

Did you notice that there are still ellipses in your file? That's is because you are simply redirecting the host output to a file.

Any output that would be written to the host can be redirected; you can append the chevrons to the end of a pipe for example:

```
Get-Process | Sort-Object -Property CPU -Descending >
C:\process.txt
```

Remember that the stream is redirected to a file but still formatted it as it would appear on the screen. You might still see the ellipses we discussed earlier in Format-Table -AutoSize.

Wait, we talked about specified streams, didn't we? Well, it is possible to redirect one or more streams to a file. The streams are:

Stream #	Description	Write Cmdlet
1	**Success** Stream	Write-Output
2	**Error** Stream	Write-Error
3	**Warning** Stream	Write-Warning
4	**Verbose** Stream	Write-Verbose
5	**Debug** Stream	Write-Debug
6	**Information** Stream	Write-Information

As an example, you might want to write errors to a log file rather than displaying them on screen. Let's write a command that will generate an error and redirect the error to a file:

```
get-item /not-here 2>> c:\temp\error.txt
```

You can also discard a stream by sending it to null

```
get-item /not-here 2> $null
```

But that is not something that I recommend you do.

Content Cmdlets

There are a number of commands that have the noun 'Content' . Check them yourself with Get-Command -Noun Content

- Add-Content – appends content to a specified item or file
- Clear-Content – deletes the content
- Get-Content – reads the content
- Set-Content – replaces the content in a file

However, you need to take care when using these cmdlets as you can get some unexpected results.

The two cmdlets you use to send output to a file are Set-Content and Add-Content. Both cmdlets convert the objects you pass in the pipeline to strings, and then output these strings to the specified file.

Be careful, if you pass either of these cmdlets a non-string object, then the object's ToString() method will be used to convert the object to a string before outputting it to the file. In many cases the ToString() method prints out the objects type.

Try it:

```
Get-Process | Set-Content -Path C:\temp\process.txt
```

The resulting file content will look like this:

System.Diagnostics.Process (ActiveConsole)
System.Diagnostics.Process (aesm_service)
System.Diagnostics.Process (ApplicationFrameHost)
System.Diagnostics.Process (armsvc)
System.Diagnostics.Process (atmgr)
System.Diagnostics.Process (audiodg)

Probably not what you were looking for right?

Out-File

The Out-File cmdlet sends output to a file.

```
Get-Process | Out-File -FilePath c:\temp\process.txt
```

The cmdlet, uses PowerShell's formatting system to write to the file rather than using the ToString() method. Using this cmdlet means PowerShell sends the output that would normally be displayed on-screen to the file. Like:-

Handles	NPM(K)	PM(K)	WS(K)	CPU(s)	Id	SI	ProcessName
386	19	11456	23984		8540	0	ActiveConsole
197	14	2828	12332		7764	0	aesm_service

If the file specified in the -path parameter does not exist, it will be created. By default. It will also overwrite an existing file. To prevent overwriting an existing file use the switch parameter -NoClobber

Remember that the Out-File cmdlet sends the data formatted as it would be at the terminals screen. Let's re-use an earlier command and send it to a file:

```
Get-Service -Name B* |
Format-Table -Property Name, RequiredServices,
CanShutDown, CanStop, DisplayName -Autosize |
Out-File C:\temp\service.txt
```

Now open the file and scroll right – the ellipses are back

```
CanShutdown CanStop DisplayName
----------- ------- -----------
      False   False GameDVR and Broadcast User Servi...
      False    True BitLocker Drive Encryption Service
      False    True Base Filtering Engine
      False   False Background Intelligent Transfer ...
```

Width

When writing output to a file using either Out-File or the redirection operators (> and >>) PowerShell formats output as a table based on the width of the console it is running within.

By default, launching PowerShell using the methods mentioned at the start of this book will default the console width to 80. So, when logging table output to file, the output in the file is truncated to 80 characters:

The Out-File cmdlet supports a -Width parameter that allows you to set the width you would like. Try it out, no ellipses this time around:

```
Get-Service -Name B* |
Format-Table -Property Name, RequiredServices,
CanShutDown, CanStop, DisplayName -Autosize |
Out-File C:\temp\service.txt -Width 200
```

When writing scripts, you should be mindful that the console width may already have been changed on the machine that it is being run. So, whilst it may look fine in your development environment it may look different 'in the wild'.

$PSDefaultParameterValue

PowerShell has a special variable $PSDefaultParameterValues that sis hashtable (more on those later) which allows you to overwrite default values of parameters used in cmdlets.

The full scope of $PSDefaultParameterValues is not a topic for this beginners' guide but it is worth calling out that you can set the default value of the Width parameter for all invocation of Out-File and the redirection operators (> and >>) for the current PowerShell Session.

To set the default -Width parameter, set the value as follows:

```
$PSDefaultParameterValues['out-file:width'] = 1000
```

Remember, this is not persistent. When you close the PowerShell session, it will rest next time you launch PowerShell. If you need to clear it before the end of the current session, you can use the command

```
$PSDefaultParameterValues.Remove('out-file:width')
```

In some cases, you will need to pipe the output to Format-Table -AutoSize before outputting to file in order for the additional width to be applied.

Export-CSV

The Export-CSV cmdlet converts PowerShell objects into a CSV string and saves them into a CSV file.

```
Get-Service | Export-CSV -Path C:\temp\service.csv -NoTypeInformation
```

Export-CSV will overwrite existing files by default. Use -Append to add data to the end of an existing file or -NoClobber to fail if an existing file exists.

The switch -NoTypeInformation removes the #TYPE information header from the output. It became the default in PowerShell 6.0 but is still supported for backwards compatibility. You will often see it in scripts found on the internet.

Check your knowledge

How do you get rid of ellipses in output?

Why does Set-Content only work well for String output?

What's the difference between Format-Table and Format-List?

When would you use the -Width parameter in your script?

What is the difference between > and >>

Working With Dates

Topics covered in this section

- Get-Date
- Date Calculations

At the end of this section, you will be able to

- Find the current date
- Calculate future of past dates
- Convert a string to a date

Working with Dates and Times in PowerShell is a very common requirement. Your script might require simple or complex date calculations for functions such as archiving or determining the range of data to operate on.

Get-Date

The first cmdlet you will probably use when working with dates and times in PowerShell is the Get-Date command. By running Get-Date with no parameters you will output a DateTime object with the current date and time.

```
$today = Get-Date
```

Get-Date uses your computer's culture settings to determine how the output is formatted. To view your computer's settings, use

```
(Get-Culture).DateTimeFormat
```

There are various date formats available in Powershell

- **d:** Denotes ShortDate
- **D:** Denotes LongDate
- **f:** Denotes long date, short time
- **F:** Denotes long date, long time
- **t:** Denotes Short time format
- **T:** Denotes Long time format
- **m, M:** Month Day format
- **g:** Denotes general data time short format
- **G:** Denotes general data time long format
- **Y or y:** Denotes Year month pattern

They can be used as part of the Get-Date -Format parameter as in

```
Get-Date -Format d
```

Compare them all with the command

```
$format = 'd','D','f','F','t','T','m','M','g','G','Y','y'
$format | ForEach-Object {Get-Date -Format $_ }
```

You can also specify the exact format to return such as:

```
Get-Date -Format MMMM/dd/yyyy
```

Be aware that by formatting the date, you now get a String returned rather than a DateTime object.

That is important to remember as you need to finish any DateTime calculation before formatting for display.

Let's look at the properties of the DateTime object

```
Get-Date | Get-Member -MemberType Property
```

TypeName: System.DateTime

Name	MemberType	Definition
Date	Property	datetime Date {get;}
Day	Property	int Day {get;}
DayOfWeek	Property	System.DayOfWeek DayOfWeek {get;}
DayOfYear	Property	int DayOfYear {get;}
Hour	Property	int Hour {get;}
Kind	Property	System.DateTimeKind Kind {get;}
Millisecond	Property	int Millisecond {get;}
Minute	Property	int Minute {get;}
Month	Property	int Month {get;}
Second	Property	int Second {get;}
Ticks	Property	long Ticks {get;}
TimeOfDay	Property	timespan TimeOfDay {get;}
Year	Property	int Year {get;}

Any of these properties can therefore be referenced using the dot (.) notation such as:

```
(Get-Date).Year
(Get-Date).DayOfWeek
```

Pay attention to the MemberType – DayOfWeek looks like a string on the screen but is a System.DayOfWeek data type.

Now check out the methods supported:

```
(Get-Date).DayOfWeek | Get-Member -MemberType Method
```

Calculating Dates

Do the same for the date System.DateTime object

```
Get-Date | Get-Member -MemberType Method
```

The first few methods are:

Name	MemberType	Definition
Add	Method	datetime Add(timespan value)
AddDays	Method	datetime AddDays(double value)
AddHours	Method	datetime AddHours(double value)
AddMilliseconds	Method	datetime AddMilliseconds(double value)
AddMinutes	Method	datetime AddMinutes(double value)
AddMonths	Method	datetime AddMonths(int months)
AddSeconds	Method	datetime AddSeconds(double value)

Let's look at the AddDays method. To calculate a date a week in advance, you could use

```
$nextWeek = (Get-Date).AddDays(7)
```

But there is not SubtractDays method? That's OK as the number of days to add can be a negative value, so to calculate the date last week use

```
$lastWeek = (Get-Date).AddDays(-7)
```

Try out the other methods like AddHours, AddMonths etc.

Comparing Dates

As well as calculating dates by adding and subtracting days, hours, minutes, milliseconds, you can create a DateTime object from a text string.

```
$newDate = [DateTime]"2020-01-03"
```

PowerShell on my laptop converts the string to a DateTime value of

03 January 2020 00:00:00

Using the Parse or ParseExact cmdlet, you can validate the input string and also determine how the date is interpreted. So, when I instead use this

```
$newDate = [DateTime]::ParseExact('2020-01-03', 'yyyy-dd-MM', $null)
```

The date is now 01 March 2020 00:00:00

So, you need to take care when converting dates to ensure that they are interpreted in the way that you meant them to be. DateTime objects can be directly compared using any of the equality operators (-eq, -lt, -le, -ge etc.)

```
If ($newDate -lt $today){
    Write-Host -Object "Something happened in the past"
}
```

You can also calculate the difference between two dates using the cmdlet New-TimeSpan.

```
New-TimeSpan [[-Start] <System.DateTime>] [[-End]
<System.DateTime>] [<CommonParameters>]
```

For example:

```
$StartDate=(GET-DATE)
$EndDate=[datetime]"01/01/2010 00:00"
NEW-TIMESPAN -Start $StartDate -End $EndDate
```

The result returned is a timespan Object

TypeName: System.TimeSpan

```
Name              MemberType Definition
----              ---------- ----------
Days              Property   int Days {get;}
Hours             Property   int Hours {get;}
Milliseconds      Property   int Milliseconds {get;}
Minutes           Property   int Minutes {get;}
Seconds           Property   int Seconds {get;}
Ticks             Property   long Ticks {get;}
TotalDays         Property   double TotalDays {get;}
TotalHours        Property   double TotalHours {get;}
TotalMilliseconds Property   double TotalMilliseconds {get;}
TotalMinutes      Property   double TotalMinutes {get;}
TotalSeconds      Property   double TotalSeconds {get;}
```

Note that when the End Date is earlier than the Start Date, the values returned are negative. Simply swap the dates around if you prefer positive integers for your calculations.

So, to get a positive integer that represents the number of days between two dates, simply use the dot notation to return the value from the property Days:

```
$EndDate=(GET-DATE)
$StartDate=[datetime]"01/01/2010 00:00"
$noDays = (NEW-TIMESPAN -Start $StartDate -End
$EndDate).Days
$noDays
```

The variable $noDays is a positive integer type Int32.

The final thing to call out on dates, is to be aware of the daylight-saving times. You can use the IsDaylightSavingTime property to check if it is daylight saving time on a computer

```
(Get-Date).IsDayLightSavingTime()
```

Be careful when comparing times between UTC and Daylight-Saving time.

Check your knowledge

What cmdlet would you se to get the current date?

What operators can you use to compare dates?

How would you calculate the date 2 weeks ago?

Why might you use ParseExact?

How would you convert text to a date?

Working with Text

Working with text in PowerShell is relatively simple. That said, there are very few cmdlets. Check it out

```
Get-Command -Noun String
```

Fortunately, the String Object supports a lot of methods.

```
$text = "text"
$text | Get-Member -Membertype Method
```

That is quite a list right. Let's look at some of the more common methods that you are likely to want to use as you beginning to write brilliant PowerShell scripts.

Concatenating Strings

The simplest way to join two strings together is with the plus operator (+)

```
$stringOne = "Hello"
$StringTwo = "World"
$stringOne + $StringTwo
```

But hold on, we want a space between them.

```
$stringOne + ' ' +  $StringTwo
```

In fact, you don't even need the plus operator here. You can concatenate strings by simply wrapping them in double quotes

```
"$stringOne  $StringTwo"
```

The double-quote method also works to join strings held in a string array

```
$WordArray = @('Hello','World')
"$WordArray"
```

Another option for concatenating strings is the *join* operator. In its simplest form, the join operator looks a little odd as the operator comes before the strings to concatenate, which are separated with a comma:

```
-join ($stringOne, $StringTwo)
```

Once again, this way of joining strings runs one into the next. If you want to specify a separator then move the -join operator after the strings and add the separator, we will use a space again.

```
$stringOne, $StringTwo -join " "
```

Splitting strings

To split a string into smaller chunks, you can use either the split method or the split operator. The former is simpler and only allows for use of explicit delimiters; the operator, on the other hand, supports regular expressions (more about those later).

```
$longString = "Hello World"
$longString.split(' ')
```

You can select more than one character to split on

```
$longString = "Hello {World} How Are You?"
$longString.split("{,}")
```

You can specify the maximum number of substrings to split into. Try it:

```
$longString = "Hello {World} How Are You?"
$longString.split("{,}",2)
```

PowerShell will stop slitting once the corresponding number of elements has been reached.

Extracting substrings

If you have used Excel before then you may have used the MID() method to extract a substring from within a longer string specifying the start position and length of the substring. PowerShell does not have a MID method but you can achieve the same thing using Substring.

```
Substring(int startIndex)
```

Retrieves a substring from this instance. The substring starts at a specified character position and continues to the end of the string.

```
("Stuck in the middle with you ").Substring(6)
```

Whereas:

```
Substring(int startIndex, int length)
```

Retrieves a substring from this instance. The substring starts at a specified character position and has a specified length.

```
("Stuck in the middle with you ").Substring(6,13)
```

Remember that PowerShell starts counting at zero (0), technically this is an offset value so the first character position has an offset of 0 – so the 'I' of 'in' is character 6 (position 7).

You can also remove a substring and return the remainder using the remove method.

```
("Stuck in the middle with you ").Remove(6,14)
```

The inverse of Remove is Insert. Try:

```
("Stuck with you").Insert(5," here")
```

To eliminate leading or trailing spaces, you can use TrimStart, TrimEnd, or Trim. Try this code to create a variable with two leading, and 1 trailing space and compare the lengths of different trims.

```
$spacePacked = "  This has leading and trailing spaces "
$spacePacked.Length
$spacePacked.TrimStart().Length
$spacePacked.TrimEnd().Length
$spacePacked.trim().Length
```

The inverse of Trim is pad and PowerShell supports PadLeft and Padright to add leading or trailing spaces to make a field a fixed length.

```
$shortString = "7-chars"
$shortString.Length
$shortString = $shortString.Padleft(10)
$shortString.length
```

Try that again with PadRight

Searching and replacing characters

PowerShell supports a variety of techniques to find and replace substrings.

Replace is the simplest method to find and replace a string literal.

```
("Hello World").Replace("World","Everyone")
```

StartsWith and *EndsWith* determine whether a string begins or ends with a certain character or string, respectively. Likewise, *Contains* tells you if a string contains a certain substring. So the following would return Boolean true.

```
("Hello world").Contains("world")
```

As would:

```
("Hello world").StartsWith("Hello")
```

```
("Hello world").EndsWith("world")
```

Note that these methods are case sensitive. To make case insensitive, add a qualifier to force ignore case.

```
("Hello
world").StartsWith("hello","CurrentCultureIgnoreCase")
```

Use Indexof to calculate the character position where a substring appears.

```
IndexOf(string value, int startIndex)
```

Reports the index of the first occurrence of the specified string in this instance. The search starts at a specified character position if one is specified.

```
("Hello world").IndexOf("world")
```

Remembering again that offset numbering in PowerShell starts at 0.

For the more demanding tasks, regular expressions are available. Regular expressions or regex are covered later.

Comparing strings

String objects can be compared using the same comparison operators as numbers when trying to determine equality. So -eq and -ne and -like (which supports wildcards). So, the following code returns Boolean true.

```
("Hello World") -Like "hello*"
```

String objects also support the CompareTo Method for comparison. If the first string is "bigger" than the second string (that is, if it comes first in the sort order), the cmdlet returns 1; if the first string is smaller, the result is -1. If the two strings are the sane then 0 is returned.

```
# Returns -1
("Hello"). CompareTo("Hello" + " " + "world")
# Returns 1
("Hello world").CompareTo("Hello" + " " + "wor")
# Returns 0
("Hello world").CompareTo("Hello" + " " + "world")
```

As well as checking equality using the -eq operator, the string object also supports Equals() as a method.

```
# Returns true
("Hello world").Equals("Hello" + " " + "world")
```

Check your knowledge

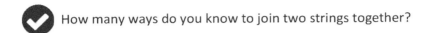 How many ways do you know to join two strings together?

 What method do you use to extract a substring from a longer string?

✔ What method would you use to left pad a field with spaces?

✔ Which operators can be used with strings?

✔ How would you check if a string starts with the text "Hello"?

Working with Arrays

Topics covered in this section

- Creating an array
- Array Index
- Adding and removing Items from an array
- Hashtables

At the end of this section, you will be able to

- Create and hols objects in an array
- Reference array objects using the offset index
- Create and use Hashtables

An array is a data structure that holds a collection of multiple objects. You can iterate through items in an array the array or reference individual objects using the array's index.

Creating an Array

To create an empty array, use the @() notation when declaring a variable

```
$arrayValues = @()
```

Arrays support the method getType(). Try it:

```
$arrayValues.GetType()
```

Will return:

```
IsPublic IsSerial Name              BaseType
-------- -------- ----              --------
True     True     Object[]          System.Array
```

129

If you want to, you can seed values as you create the array. Values are separated with a comma.

```
$newArray = @(10,20,30)
```

Note that asperand or 'at symbol' (@) is optional so

```
$otherArray = 40,50,60
```

usually works just as well.

You can also use splatting technique to define the variable values over multiple lines without the need for commas. Like:

```
$thirdArray = @(
100
200
300
400 )
```

If you are creating an array that contains text strings, then each value needs to be enclosed in quotes:

```
$textArray = 'one','two','three'
```

When you call the variable, all items are returned to the pipline (an in the absence of another command after a pipe, to the console screen). So

```
$thirdArray
```

Returns

```
100
200
300
400
```

To access individual items in the array, you use squared brackets [] with an offset value. So, to access the first item in an array, use the value 0 as you want no offset

```
$thirdArray[0]
```

The second item would have offset of 1, the third an offset of 2 etc.

To get the value of the last item in an array you can use the special offset value -1

```
$thirdArray[-1]
```

To count how many items are in an array look at the array's Count property

```
$thirdArray.Count
```

PowerShell also allows you to select more than one offset value at a time, for example to get the first and third value use:

```
$thirdArray[0,2]
```

You can also call arrange of values:

```
$thirdArray[0..2]
```

If you use an offset that would make the item out of bounds, e.g. calling the fourth item in your array of three, PowerShell simply returns a null. Let's prove it,

```
$thirdArray[9] -eq $null
```

Returns True as there are only four objects int the array, so when asking for the object with offset of nine (i.e. the tenth object) nothing is returned.

So far you have been adding simple string and values to you arrays, but an array can contain any object. For example, you can pipe a list of all processes running on your device to an array:

```
$proc = Get-Process
```

Well done, you have created your first associative array, or hashtable. We will cover them in more depth later.

Adding Items to an Array

As you have seen values can be seeded to an array on creation, either explicitly or by piping output to a new array. You can also overwrite the content of an array by just recreating it again with new values.

```
$array = 10,20,30
$array = 100,200,300
$array
```

You can also amend the value of each item in an array using its offset index

```
$array[0] = 1000
```

But you cannot add a new item using an index greater than the last existing value as that would return an error 'Index was outside the bounds of the array'.

```
# returns outside the bounds error
$array[3] = 400
```

In the example above, an error is returned as you are trying to add a value into the array object with offset three, the fourth object, but there are only three objects in the array.

To add a new value into an array, use one of the following constructs (examples shown add two new values 400 and 500 to the existing array):

```
# +=
$array += 400,500
```

```
# +
$array = $array + 400,500
```

```
# add an array
$newValue = 400,500
$array += $newValue
```

Deleting Items from an Array

Let's try to delete a value from the array,

```
$array = $array -200
```

will fail with an error

```
Method invocation failed because [System.Object[]] does
not contain a method named 'op_Subtraction'
```

This error tells you that there is no subtraction method. So you need to look at the methods available and find one suitable for deleting an object from the array.

You have been piping objects to the Get-Member cmdlet to find the methods supported. But once you have objects inside of your array, the pipeline will pass the member objects inside your array and not of the array itself so this method will not work.

```
$array | Get-Member
```

Returns the methods and properties of the type System.Int32 as those are the objects that we added to the array. Instead, you must use the -InputObject parameter of the get-member cmdlet.

```
Get-Member -InputObject $array
```

That shows that the System.Object[] supports the method remove. So why is it that you get an error when you try

```
$array.Remove(200)
```

The remove fails as the array is fixed size (confusing isn't it, fixed size but I can add items and extend the size but not reduce it? Well actually when you add a value, you recreate the array with a new fixed size).

So to remove a value from an array, you need to create a new array without the item you want to remove. If the value is unique, you can exclude it by reference to its value in a ForEach-Object loop.

```
$newArray = @()
$array | ForEach-Object {
    If ($_ -ne 200) {
        $newarray += $_
    }
}
```

Or alternately you can make the new array by referencing only the offset index of the items to include like so:

```
$array = 100,200,300,400,500,600
$newArray = $array[0,2,3,4,5]
```

Best to avoid the need to remove values at all.

Strongly typed arrays

So far You have created arrays that can hold any type of object, even mixing types of objects in one array.

```
$mixedArray = 1, 2, 3
$mixedArray += 'four'
$mixedArray.type()
```

Notice how Get-Member now returns the members for both Int32 and String?

When you create a strongly typed array, it can only contain values or objects of the specified type.

```
[int[]] $numberArray = 1,2,3
```

Trying to add a string value to this array will return an error

```
# Cannot convert value "four" to type "System.Int32"
$NumberArray += 'four'
```

Only use strongly types arrays where you want to control the types of objects that can be held and have good error handling in place.

Nested arrays

An array inside an array is called a nested array.

```
$nestArray = @(@(1,2,3),@(4,5,6),@(7,8,9))
```

When you call the array variable it returns all of the values so it is not immediately obvious that it is nested

$nestArray

```
1
2
3
4
5
6
7
8
9
```

But using the index shows multiple values inside of each item

$nestArray[0]

```
1
2
3
```

Hashtable

A hashtable, or associative array, looks like an ordinary array, except you store each value is stored alongside its key. To create an empty hashtable uses braces instead of parentheses.

$hashTable = @{}

And check its object type

$hashtable.GetType()

```
IsPublic IsSerial Name                    BaseType
-------- -------- ----                    --------
True     True     Hashtable               System.Object
```

Piping the empty hashtable to get-Member cmdlet shows it has a type of TypeName: System.Collections.Hashtable

You can also seed values when creating the hashtable. Let's create a hashtable containing some basic information about people:

```
$hashtable = @{Name = 'John'; Age = 30; EyeColor = "Blue"}
```

The hashtable object supports the Add method to add additional keys.

```
$hashtable.Add('HairColor','brown')
```

The hashtable also supports the Remove method to delete a key

```
$hashtable.Remove('HairColor')
```

Hashtables can also be nested. That means values can be held as a hashtable within a hashtable. Let's continue with our list of people

```
$people = @{
    Graham = @{
        Age   = 30
         EyeColor = 'Blue'
           HairColor = 'Brown'
    }
    Hollie = @{
        Age   = 25
         EyeColor = 'Green'
           HairColor = 'Blonde'
    }
}
```

You can see that now we start to build up a data structure that is looking a little like a database. Trouble is, it gets a little harder to read the values. Calling the hashtable:

$people

Returns:

Name	Value
Hollie	{HairColor, Age, EyeColor}
Graham	{HairColor, Age, EyeColor}

But now we can use the .dot properties, so to find Graham's Age

$people.Graham.Age

Alternately just walk the list using ForEach

```
foreach($name in $people.keys) {
    $person = $people[$name]
    '{0}, age {1}, has {2} hair and {3} eyes' -f $name,
    $person.age, $person.HairColor, $person.EyeColor
}
```

Will return

Hollie, age 25, has Blonde hair and Green eyes
Graham, age 30, has Brown hair and Blue eyes

Alternately, if nested Hashtables are not for you, you could hold an array of Hashtables instead.

```
$people=@(
    @{name= 'Graham';Age = 30 ; EyeColor = 'Blue'},
    @{name= 'Hollie';Age = 25 ; EyeColor = 'Green'}
 )
```

Now you can query the array to return all of the details for an individual with a simple filter (more on filtering in the next section):

$people | Where-Object Name -like "Hollie"

Check your knowledge

What is the difference between an array and a hashtable?

How would you add a value to an array?

What is a nested array?

How can you remove an item from an array?

What is a strongly typed array?

What type of array would the following command produce?

```
$arrType = @{}
```

Sorting, Filtering & Measuring

Topics covered in this section

- Sorting Objects
- Filtering and selecting objects and values
- Measuring objects

  At the end of this section you will be able to

- Control the order of output
- Select only the objects or values that you want
- Be able to measure objects

Sort-Object

There is no guarantee as to the order of objects that a cmdlet will return objects in PowerShell. If you want to be able to control the order in which objects are sent in the pipeline, use the cmdlet Sort-Object.

The syntax for the cmdlet is

```
Sort-Object [[-Property] <Object[]>] [-Descending] [-
Unique] [-InputObject <psobject>] [-Culture <string>] [-
CaseSensitive]  [<CommonParameters>]
```

Remember the parameter -InputObject means that Sort-Object cmdlet will accept input from the pipeline. So, the easiest way to sort any list of objects is to pipe the output to Sort-Object:

`Get-Process | Sort-Object`

If you do not specify the value to sort on, Sort-Object will sort on the default value – in the case of Process that is the name.

You can change the value to sort on, for example to sort on the amount of memory used based on the Working set (WS) size:

```
Get-Process | Sort-Object -Property WS
```

Ok, but you probably want to sort descending to show the busiest processes first:

```
Get-Process | Sort-Object -Property WS -Descending
```

You can also sort on multiple properties:

```
Get-Process | Sort-Object -Property WS, Name -Descending
```

And you can also sort on multiple properties mixing ascending and descending sort order

```
Get-Process | Sort-Object -property  @{Expression = "WS";
Descending = $true}, @{Expression = "Name"; Descending =
$false}
```

Use the get-help cmdlet for more information on the advanced parameters of the Sort-Object cmdlet. A couple more interesting cases are the -Unique switch to return only unique values

```
Get-Process | Sort-Object -Property Name -Unique
```

And -CaseSensitive to make the sort case sensitive – by default it is case insensitive.

Select-Object

The Select-Object cmdlet selects specified properties of an object or set of objects. It accepts input from the pipeline and so can be used thus:

```
Get-Process | select-Object -Property Name, Id
```

It can be used to only return a sub-set of properties for an object and to change the order in which they are returned as in the above example.

It can also select unique objects, a specified number of objects, or objects in a specified position in an array.

To select unique objects

```
Get-Process | select-Object -Property Name -Unique
```

To include only the first or last n objects:

```
# First 5
Get-Process | Select-Object -First 5

# Last 5
Get-process | Select-Object -Last 5
```

You can also skip the first n objects

```
# Skip first 10 objects
Get-process | Select-Object -Skip 10
```

or skip the last n objects

```
# Skip last 10 records
Get-process | Select-Object -SkipLast 10
```

Or return the object which matches the offset index - remember the first object has offset index of zero [0].

```
# return 16th object – offset of 15
Get-process | Select-Object -Index 15
```

Select-Object has an alias 'Select' hence you will often see it referenced in the shorthand alias form when viewing scripts online. So, the above example may be rewritten as

```
Get-process | Select -Index 15
```

The alias for any command can be found in Get-help and conversely you can get help for the alias to return the full cmdlet name

```
Get-Help gps
```

Where-Object

The Where-Object cmdlet selects only those objects that have particular property values from the collection of objects that are passed to it. There are two ways that it can be used.

Firstly, as a straightforward comparison statement:

```
Get-Service | Where-Object -Property StartType -EQ
'Automatic'
```

Add a select statement to check that it only filtered objects with the correct StartType

```
Get-Service | Where-Object -Property StartType -EQ
'Automatic'| Select Name, Status, StartType
```

Or secondly as a script block that allows more complex queries to be written:

```
Get-Service |
Where-Object {($_.Status -notcontains 'Running') -and
($_.StartType -eq 'Manual')}
```

Notice that the script block is wrapped in braces {} and the individual comparators to be strung together with an -AND statement are enclosed in brackets ().

Filter Parameter

Many cmdlets accept -Filter as a parameter.

The -filter parameter accepts a script block of PowerShell Expressions Language Syntax that accepts comparison operators. So as an example, to find a user in Active Directory (with the AD module loaded) you might use:

```
Get-Aduser -Filter {Name -Like 'John Doe'}
```

Group-Object

The Group-Object cmdlet displays objects in groups based on the value of the specified property. Group-Object returns a table with one row for each property value and a column that displays the number of items with that value.

Try the following example. First let's get all services and put them into an array:

```
$services = Get-Service
```

Check out the array content, quite a list. Now let's group them but not specify what to group on.

```
$services | Group-Object
```

The output gives a count and a single field with all services running. Not much help. So now let's group on multiple properties selecting the Status to show running and stopped services and by the StartType.

```
$services = get-service | group status,starttype
```

Now it's looking more like an interesting grouped list but it's hard to see what's in each list as the group is shown in a single field.

```
Count Name                        Group
----- ----                        -----
  156 Stopped, Manual             {AarSvc_5b8d2cf, AarSvc_5c9777f, AJRouter, ALG...}
   67 Running, Automatic          {AdobeARMservice, AudioEndpointBuilder, Audiosrv, BFE...}
   48 Running, Manual             {Appinfo, Browser, BthAvctpSvc, camsvc...}
    6 Stopped, Automatic          {edgeupdate, gpsvc, gupdate, MapsBroker...}
    7 Stopped, Disabled           {NetTcpPortSharing, RemoteAccess, RemoteRegistry, shpamsvc...}
```

You can, of course, now pipe the array to Where-Object cmdlet to select one of the groups and pipe that again to Select-Object and use the parameter -ExpandProperty to display the group in full.

```
$services | Where-Object name -eq 'Stopped, Disabled' |
Select-Object -ExpandProperty Group
```

You are now starting to combine multiple cmdlets with the pipeline without even thinking about it, look how far you have come from the start of the book.

Measure-Object

The Measure-Object cmdlet performs calculations on the property values of objects. You can use Measure-Object to count objects or count objects with a specified Property. You can also use Measure-Object to calculate the Minimum, Maximum, Sum, Standard Deviation and Average of numeric values. For String objects, you can use Measure-Object to count the number of lines, words, and characters.

For example, let's use measure-Object with the piped output of get-ChildItem, which when used with no parameters returns the items in the current folder. So navigate to c:\users\<<username>>\documents and then type:

```
Get-ChildItem | Measure-Object -Property length -Minimum
-Maximum -Sum -Average
```

This command displays the Minimum, Maximum, and Sum of the sizes of all files in the current directory, and the average size of a file in the directory. What is returned should look something like this:

```
Count   : 51
Average : 876667.176470588
Sum     : 44710026
Maximum : 20866348
Minimum : 37
Property : length
```

By selecting the value required, you can use measure-Object to return min or max values from an array like this:

```
$intArray = 1,2,300,400,5,0
($intArray | Measure-Object -Minimum).Minimum
($intArray | Measure-Object -Maximum).Maximum
```

When working with files, you can use measure-Object to count the lines, words and characters in a file.

```
Get-Content C:\temp\test.txt | Measure-Object -Line -Word
-Character
```

Add the switch –IgnoreWhiteSpace to ignore white space in character counts. By default, white space is not ignored.

Other Properties

You can also use the objects properties to find out more about the object. Remember, you can use the get-member cmdlet to find an object's properties; here are a few to remember:

```
# String has length property
$stringvar =  'hello World'
$stringVar.length


# Array has a count
$array = 1,2,3,4,5
$array.Count
```

Check your knowledge

How many ways do you know to restrict the Objects returned in a query?

How would you find cmdlets that have the -Filter Parameter?

Can you group on more than one property?

What command would you use to find the number of objects in an array?

What can measure-Object be used for?

Error Handling

In general, there are two types of error in PowerShell. Terminating and Non-Terminating Errors. Terminating errors will cause the current script block to stop and return an error to the host. A terminating error can be handled with a Try Catch command block.

How Non-Terminating errors are handles is controlled by a preference variable $ErrorActionPreference. The default it to Continue which means that execution will continue to the next command. Non-terminating errors cannot be handled with a Try-Catch block.

Try – Catch
Use try, catch, and finally blocks are used to respond to or handle terminating errors in scripts. In the simplest form the syntax is

```
try {<statement list>}
catch {<statement list>}
```

and optionally followed by

```
finally {<statement list>}
```

For example:

```
$err = 100/0
```

Will return an error as division by zero is an illegal operation.

You can catch the error in a try-catch block and return a friendly error and continue processing your script:

```
#catch a div by zero error
Try {
    $err = 100/0 }
Catch {
    Write-Host -Object "An Error Occurred but we will
continue" -backgroundColor Red }
```

If you want to include the error message use the special variable $_

```
#catch a div by zero error
Try {
    $err = 100/0 }
Catch {
    Write-Host -Object "An Error Occurred - $_ -  but we
will continue" -backgroundColor Red }
```

You can generate a terminating error in your script using the Throw command

```
throw "Terminating Error"
```

You can use catch to look only for specific types of errors.

For example, to trap a command not found error:

```
#trap command not found
Try {
    Get-MyInvalidCommand }
Catch
[System.Management.Automation.CommandNotFoundException] {
    Write-Host -Object "This command does not exist" -
backgroundColor Red }
```

Type 'powershell; about_Try_Catch_Finally in your favourite search engine for more information.

Trap

When writing script files, you can also use the Trap command to set the default error handling for the entirety of the script.

```
trap [[<error type>]] {<statement list>}
```

You can use Trap in your script to

- Display the error after processing the trap statement block and continuing execution of the script. This is the default behaviour.

```
# default
Trap {Write-Host "An error occurred script will
continue"}
```

- Display the error and abort execution of the script using break in the trap statement.

```
# Exit the script
Trap {Write-Host "An error occurred script will now
stop"; Break}
```

- Silence the error, but continue execution of the script by using continue in the trap statement.

```
#Continue Silently
Trap {Continue}
```

Check your knowledge

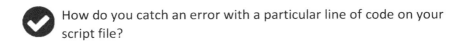 How do you catch an error with a particular line of code on your script file?

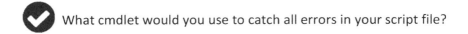 What cmdlet would you use to catch all errors in your script file?

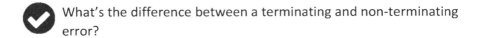 What's the difference between a terminating and non-terminating error?

Functions

Topics covered in this section

- What is a function
- Syntax of a function
- Passing data into a function

At the end of this section, you will be able to

- Write functions
- Call a function with parameters

Once you start to write more advanced PowerShell scripts, you will find yourself repeat blocks of code over and over again. Clearly this is an inefficient way of working but fortunately PowerShell supports code modularization – that it you can write blocks of code that can be reused and called time and time again.

Simple Function Syntax

In its simplest form, a function can be defined as

```
Function <<unction-name> {<code-block>}
```

For example:

```
Function Write-HW {
    Write-Host "Hello World"
}
```

This simple function is then executed by calling it by the function name

```
Write-HW
```

Looks just like a cmdlet doesn't it?

Function Parameters

Your function is likely to contain code that takes parameters as input and then processes the values. To create a parameter for a function, you need to add a param block. The param block holds all the parameters for the function.

Define a param block with the param keyword followed by parentheses:

```
Function Write-Something {
    [CmdletBinding()]
    param()
        Write-Host -Object "Hello World"
}
```

At this stage the param block is empty so the function still won't look for any parameters as input. Let's add one:

```
Function Write-Something {
    [CmdletBinding()]
    param(
    [Parameter(Mandatory)]
        [string]$message
)
        Write-Host -Object "$message"
}
```

Notice the (mandatory) statement, this is telling PowerShell that the parameter is not optional. If you call the function with no parameter (by just typing Write-Something PowerShell will prompt for them missing input.

```
Write-Something
```

cmdlet Write-Something at command pipeline position 1
Supply values for the following parameters:
message:

of course, leaving out the (mandatory) statement will make the parameter optional and your code will need to deal with the absence of any input. You can also add a default value:

```
Function Write-Something {
     [CmdletBinding()]
     param(
     [Parameter()]
          [string]$message = 'No message received'
)
          Write-Host -Object "$message"
}
```

Now if you don't supply a value for the $message variable, it will be set to 'No message received'. To supply the parameter, simply add it after the function name when calling it.

Write-Something "Hello World"

Now try again without the parameter to see the default value used:

Write-Something

Finally, you might also like to validate the values being passed to the function. This is, of course, entirely optional and you can manage validation within your code but it is shown here as an example.

```
function Install-Sware {
     param(
          [Parameter(Mandatory)]
          [ValidateSet('1','2', '2.1')]
          [string]$version
     )

   $message = "installing Software version: " + $version
   Write-Host -Object $message
}
```

Calling the function with an invalid parameter returns an ungraceful message. Try it

Install-Sware 4

Did you see the error?

Install-Sware : Cannot validate argument on parameter 'version'. The argument "4" does not belong to the set "1,2,2.1"
specified by the ValidateSet attribute. Supply an argument that is in the set and then try the command again.

You might want to wrap in a Try-Catch error handler.

These examples are all very simple, so you might be wondering when to use a function? Weill here is a simple script that I wrote to find recursively nested AD groups that is a good example of how a complicated loop can be simplified as this function calls itself.

```
function Get-NestedGroupMember    {
    param (
            [Parameter(Mandatory)]
            [string]$group
            )

    ## Find all members in the group specified
    $groups = @()
    $members = Get-ADGroupMember -Identity $group
    foreach ($member in $members)    {

    # If any member in  that group is another group just
    # call this function again
    If ($member.objectClass -eq 'group')    {
        If ($member.Name -notin $groups) {
        $group += $member.Name
          Get-NestedGroupMember -Group $member.Name   }
        } else {
        # otherwise, just  output the non-group
        # object (probably a user account)
        $member.Name
        }
  }
```

Check your knowledge

 How do you format a function with parameters?

 How can you validate parameters in your functions?

 What does the function always end with?

PSRemoting

Topics covered in this section

- Running PowerShell cmdlets on a remote machine
- WinRM & CMI

At the end of this section you will be able to

- Query a remote machine

PowerShell provides a set of features that enable you to connect to a remote machine, authenticate and remote commands. Output from the remote commands is then displayed on the local machine.

These features of PowerShell Remoting, or PSRemoring for short, allow you to run any cmdlet on one or many different remote computers. You can either simply run commands or scripts on the remote machine or establish a persistent connection.

-ComputerName

The simplest way to collect data or change settings on a remote computer is with any cmdlet that has the -ComputerName parameter. These cmdlets work without any special configuration on the remote end. To find the available cmdlets run the following command:

```
Get-Command | Where-Object {$_.parameters.keys -contains
"ComputerName" -and $_.parameters.keys -notcontains
"Session"}
```

You should see a list of commands like this:

157

```
CommandType        Name
-----------        ----
Cmdlet             Add-Computer
Cmdlet             Clear-EventLog
Cmdlet             Get-EventLog
Cmdlet             Get-HotFix
Cmdlet             Get-Process
Cmdlet             Get-PSSession
Cmdlet             Get-Service
Cmdlet             Get-WmiObject
Cmdlet             Invoke-WmiMethod
Cmdlet             Limit-EventLog
Cmdlet             New-EventLog
Cmdlet             Register-WmiEvent
Cmdlet             Remove-Computer
Cmdlet             Remove-EventLog
Cmdlet             Remove-WmiObject
Cmdlet             Rename-Computer
Cmdlet             Restart-Computer
Cmdlet             Set-Service
Cmdlet             Set-WmiInstance
Cmdlet             Show-EventLog
Cmdlet             Stop-Computer
Cmdlet             Test-Connection
Cmdlet             Write-EventLog
```

The cmdlets get objects using the underlying .Net framework methods.

Prerequisites

Other than those cmdlets listed above, most PSRemoting uses a session to connect to the remote machine. To connect a session, the remote machine must be configured for remote management.

The machine must be running

- PowerShell v3.0 +
- .Net framework v4 +
- WRM3 +

An appropriate version of .Net and WRM is included by default in Windows 8, Server 2012 and all later editions.

The user must be a member of the remote machine Administrators Group.

PSRemoting must be enabled.

To enable PSRemoting use the following cmdlet, running PowerShell as Administrator:

Enable-PSRemoting

And to check it is enabled try to start a new session (without a - computername parameter the sessions is initiated on the localhost)

New-PSSession

PSRemoting relies on WINRM (Microsoft's implementation of WSMAN) Troubleshooting issues with WIMRM and the networking or firewall requirements is beyond the scope of this beginners guide. However, to see if WINRM is running and listening, try the following command:

```
winrm e wrinrm/config/listener
```

Sessions

PSRemoting relies on sessions. A session is the remote shell that runs commands you specify on the remote machine. When you start a session, the client attempts to connect to the remote machine on a WINRM listener (a small web server). When the client connects the user is authenticated (Basic authentication, Kerberos or NTLM) and the session is initiated. Once the session is enabled, data can flow between the local and remote end (known as serialization).

Start an interactive session with a single computer using Enter-PSSession

PSSession -Computername server01

Notice how the command prompt now changes to the name of the remote machine? Any commands that you tyoe now will be executed at the remote until you exit the sessions

Exit-PSSession

You can run a command on one or more than one remote machine without an interactive session using the Invoke-Command cmdlet. When using Invoke-Command, the script block to be executed is enclosed in braces {}

```
Invoke-Command -Computername server01, server02
-ScriptBlock {#<<commands go here, separated by a semi
colon>>}
```

Similarly, it is possible to run a script on one or more remote machines using Invoke-Command

```
Invoke-Command -Computername server01,server02 -FilePath
C:\scripts\script.ps1
```

Note that the file path must be accessible to the remote machine (so choice a file share that is accessible or deploy the script first using your preferred distribution method).

It is also possible to establish a persistent connection where output from one query or cmdlet can be used as input to another. Firstly, establish the connection using New-PSSession. It is usual to assign the session to a variable

```
$sesh = New-PSSession -Computername server01,server02
```

Then run the commands referencing the session object variable

```
Invoke-Command -Session $sesh -ScriptBlock {$proc = Get-
Process}
```

As a persistent connection has been established any objects created remain available, so in the case of the example above the variable $proc can be reused in a subsequent command:

```
Invoke-Command -Session $sesh -ScriptBlock {$proc |
Where-Object {$_.name = "svchost"}}
```

The session remains open until it times out or is closed

Remove-PSSession

It is possible to have more than one session open at the same time. It is also not strictly necessary to assign the session to a variable, they can be

160

referenced by their Id. |To get a list of all available sessions initiated since the start of the current PowerShell session try:

Get-PSSession

Noe that you know how to run commands on a remote machine, we will look at the two sets of cmdlets that allow you to get data about it. PowerShell provides two sets of cmdlets for accessing data about a computer, WMI and CIM.

WMI

WMI stands for Windows Management Instrumentation. WMI is a Powerful set of PowerShell cmdlets that allows you to monitor and manage remote machines including tasks like:

- Setting security options
- Collecting information from the server metrics
- Set permissions for users and groups
- Schedule tasks
- Enable or disable event logs

Remember you can use the Get-Command cmdlet to find the commands that support WMI thus:

Get-Command -Noun WMI*

The following cmdlets should be available:

Cmdlet	Description
Get-WmiObject	Get instances of WMI classes or information about the available classes
Invoke-WmiMethod	Calls WMI methods
Register-WmiEvent	Subscribes to a WMI event
Remove-WmiObject	Deletets WMI classes and instances
Set-WmiInstance	Creates or modifies instances of WMI classes

Get-WMIObject supports the -ComputerName parameter to execute on a remote machine. Remember you can use Get-Help Get-WmiObject for more details on the syntax and parameters supported.

To get details of the operating on your machine, including its name, try

```
Get-WMIObject -Class Win32_OperatingSystem -Property Name
-ComputerName Localhost
```

Then try to replace Localhost with a remote machine name.

To find the classes available on a computer , try

```
Get-WMIObject -List| Where{$_.name -match "^Win32_"} |
Sort Name | Format-Table Name
```

The problem with WMI is the underlying network protocols that it uses (DCOM and RPC) requires a significant number of firewall ports to be open between the console being used to run the commands and the remote machines.

CIM

With the introduction of PowerShell v3, Microsoft introduced a new set of CIM based cmdlets.

You will still come across many scripts online that use WMI, and the Get-WMIObject cmdlet in particular but just beware that WMI cmdlets are being deprecated in favour of CIM commands.

Try running

```
Get-Command -Noun CIM*
```

So, to query a remote machine and find the status of all services you might have used the WMI command

```
Get-WmiObject -Class win32_service -ComputerName server01
| Select Name, State, Status
```

In PSRemoting you can achieve the same result using

```
Get-CimInstance -ClassName Win32_Service -ComputerName
server01
```

For a full list of CIM Classes to query use the cmdlet Get-CMIClass with no parameters or switches

```
Get-CIMClass -ComputerName server01
```

Did you notice the extra information returned by the CIM cmdlet above?

CIM queries can be quite inefficient as a lot of data is collected and discarded as the query executes. When using Get-CIMInstance it helps to specify the property that you want to return. For example, to return just the operating system Version you would use:

```
Get-CIMInstance -ClassName CIM_OperatingSystem -Property
Version -ComputerName Server01| Select-Object Version
```

You should also note that is you pipe this command to Get-Member you will see what is returned is TypeName:

```
Selected.Microsoft.Management.Infrastructure.CimInstance
```

If you want just to return a text string with the version number, use the ExpandProperty parameter:

```
Get-CIMInstance -ClassName CIM_OperatingSystem -Property
Version -ComputerName Server01| Select-Object -
ExpandProperty Version
```

Check the type returned this time, it should be a string.

These commands are extremely useful for a sysadmin. Imagine that you wanted to get the version of OS running on every server (forgetting that you have an asset register or cmdb) you could do that in many ways but the simplest (where you only have a few servers) might be:

```
Get-CIMInstance -ClassName CIM_OperatingSystem -Property
Version -ComputerName Server01, Server02, Serer03,
Server04, Server05 | Select-Object -ExpandProperty
Version
```

CIM cmdlets include

Cmdlet	Purpose
Get-CimInstance	Gets instances of a class.
New-CimInstance	Creates a new instance of a class.
Remove-CimInstance	Removes one of more instances of a class.
Set-CimInstance	Modifies one or more instances of a class.
Get-CimAssociatedInstance	Gets all the associated instances for a particular instance.
Invoke-CimMethod	Invokes instance or static method of a class.
Get-CimClass	Gets class schema of a CIM class.
Register-CimIndicationEvent	Helps subscribe to events.
New-CimSession	Creates a CIM Session with local or a remote machine
Get-CimSession	Gets a list of CIM Sessions that have been made.
Remove-CimSession	Removes CimSessions that are there on a machine.
New-CimSessionOption	Creates a set of options that can be used while creating a CIM session.

Table 8 CIM Commands

Remote management using PowerShell and auto-ops is a big topic that could fill a book on their own. I hope that this overview has given you enough as a beginner to begin running remote commands and has given you the confidence to try more and keep reading and investigating.

Check your knowledge

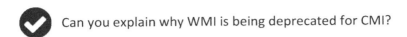 Can you explain why WMI is being deprecated for CMI?

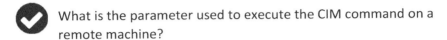 What is the parameter used to execute the CIM command on a remote machine?

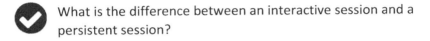 What is the difference between an interactive session and a persistent session?

Regular Expressions

Topics covered in this section

- What are regular expressions
- Simple regex syntax

  At the end of this section, you will be able to

- Describe what regular expression are
- Search for simple patterns.

Regular Expression or Regex is a topic that can be as deep as the ocean and is quite advanced for this book but we will take a look at it here and give you pointers to allow you to research more if you choose to do so.

A regular expression is a pattern used to match text. It can be made up of literal characters, operators, and other constructs.

Literals, Groups and Ranges

You can use literal numbers and characters in your patterns for exact matches when you know exactly what needs to match. For example

```
"This is a book on PowerShell" -match "book"
```

Returns True as the literal "book" is found in the string "This is a book on PowerShell".

Sometimes you need a pattern where any one of a range of digit or letters make the match valid. For example, to match the word bag, big, bog or bug you can use a character group

```
'big' -match 'b[aiou]g'
```

In the example above, the square brackets indicate a group and any letter in the group is a valid match. But hold on what about this:

```
"Mine is the biggest" –match 'b[aiou]g'
```

Where you still expecting that to return true? It did as a match was made on the first three characters of the word biggest. If you only want to match whole words, then there are several different ways to do that

You can use a word boundary \b

```
# No match
"Mine is the biggest" -match  '\bb[aiou]g\b'

# match
"Mine is the biggest bag" -match  '\bb[aiou]g\b'
```

In the example above the \b at that start and end of the text to match specifies a word boundary.

Or look for a white space character

```
"Mine is the biggest bag here" -match  '\sb[aiou]g\s'
```

But beware that will this not find a match in "Mine is the biggest bag" as there is no white space after the word bag.

You can also look for anchors, the two most common at the caret ^ and the dollar symbol $ which when used together assert that the string must match the whole of the string. For example

```
# No Match
"big bag" -match  '^b[aiou]g$'

# Match
"big"  -match '^b[aiou]g$'
```

As well as a character group, you can also use a range.

```
"big"  -match '^b[A-Z]g$'
```

[A-Z] specifies any letter between A and Z in the alphabet (upper or lower case as PowerShell is case insensitive. So this would also match BUG, BOG, bug, and nonsense strings like BFG.

[0-9] is a range to select any digit from zero to nine.

For both of these ranges there is also a shortcut using an escape character.

\d represents any digit and **\w** any a-z character. The wildcard point(.) represents any character.

Quantifiers

Quantifiers control how many instances of each element should be present in the input string. These are probably the most commonly used quantifiers available in PowerShell:

Quantifier	Description
*	Zero or more times.
+	One or more times.
?	Zero or one time.
{3}	exactly 3 times
{n,m}	At least n, but no more than m times.

Using quantifiers along with groups and wildcards, it is possible to build powerful pattern matches. For example, you might want to check a string to see if it looks like a valid email address:

```
'Southcrater@virginmedia.com' -match '\b[A-Z0-9]+@[A-Z0-9]+\.[\.A-Z0-9]+\b'
```

Returns true

I have simplified the regex here to make it easier to understand, in my production version I have included a large number of special characters in the initial group. Sometimes special characters need to be escaped. In the example above I include a match for the period or fullstop (.) in a domain name.

As the period symbol is a special character that means any character, I have to escape it with a preceding backslash \. In fact any special character will need to be proceeded with an escape character when used as a character literal.

Check Your Knowledge

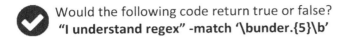 Would the following code return true or false?
"I understand regex" -match '\bunder.{5}\b'

✓ When would you need to use the escape character?

✓ What does the quantifier {2,5} mean?

Final Thoughts

I hope that you have found this book useful. If you have then please leave a positive review on the online store where you made your purchase – we are a small indie publishing company and online reviews help us a lot. If you find errors or have suggestions for future edits please tell us, our email address is southcrater@virginmedia.com

You will note read a lot about the use of Write-Host as you continue learning about PowerShell. Prior to v5.x of PowerShell the cmdlet Write-Host was considered dangerous to use. Write-Output was favoured but I have kept it simple in this book for beginners.

As you develop your style and reads more online scripts, you will come across shorthand PowerShell. Most commands have one or more alias that can be used to reduce keystrokes as you type your scripts. So, Format-List becomes FL and you no longer name parameters but trust PowerShell will interpret them based on the parameter position. It is quite common for shorthand PowerShell to be used but I have used longhand cmdlet calls in this book and would encourage you to do the same.

Good luck on your journey, I hope you enjoy PowerShell scripting as much as I have.

Made in United States
Orlando, FL
06 May 2022

17601317R00104